On
Philology

On Philology

Edited by Jan Ziolkowski

The Pennsylvania State University Press
University Park and London

This work was originally published as a special-focus issue of *Comparative Literature Studies* (vol. 27, no. 1, 1990) entitled "What is Philology?" consisting of proceedings from the conference "What is Philology?" sponsored by the Center for Literary and Cultural Studies, Harvard University, March 1988. The issue is reproduced in its entirety with the exception of the book reviews.

Library of Congress Cataloging-in-Publication Data
On philology / edited by Jan Ziolkowski
      p. cm.
   "Originally published as a special-focus issue of Comparative literature studies (vol. 27, no. 1, 1990) . . . consisting of proceedings from the conference 'What is Philology?' sponsored by the Center for Literary and Cultural Studies, Harvard University, March 1988"—T.p. verso.
   ISBN 0-271-00716-8 (alk. paper)
   1. Philology. I. Ziolkowski, Jan. II. Harvard University.
Center for Literary and Cultural Studies.
P121.05 1990
400 — dc20   90-7579

It is the policy of The Pennsylvania State University Press to use acid-free paper for the first printing of all clothbound books. Publications on uncoated stock satisfy the minimum requirements of American National Standard for Information Sciences — Permanence of Paper for Printed Library Materials, ANSI Z39.48-1984.

CONTENTS

"What is Philology": Introduction
Jan Ziolkowski   1

Philology
Wendell Clausen   13

The Case for Medieval Philology
Eckehard Simon   16

What is Philology?
Calvert Watkins   21

Philology: What is at Stake?
Barbara Johnson   26

Thoughts on Celtic Philology and Philologists
John T. Koch   31

Death of a Schoolboy: The Early Greek Beginning of a Crisis in
     Philology
Gregory Nagy   37

Anti-Foundational Philology
Jonathan Culler   49

Greek Philology: Diversity and Difference
Margaret Alexiou   53

Philology as Subversion: The Case of Afro-America
Carolivia Herron   62

Past and Future in Classical Philology
Richard F. Thomas   66

Philology's Discontents: Response
Stephen Owen   75

"What is Philology?"
Introduction

JAN ZIOLKOWSKI

This special issue of *Comparative Literature Studies* brings together talks, some extensively revised, others virtually unchanged, that were delivered at a conference entitled "What is Philology?" The gathering took place on Saturday, March 19, 1988 at Harvard University under the aegis of the Center for Literary and Cultural Studies. The depth and breadth of interest in the conference was deeply gratifying. I had not experienced another occasion when so many scholars from different language and literature departments gathered at Harvard, and I hope that publishing the proceedings will benefit a larger community outside the University.

By way of introduction I will describe how the event originated. My description will explore a few of the reasons why an interdisciplinary conference of a dozen speakers and respondents attracted an audience of more than two hundred, and why a topic that may sound rarefied drew participants whose main fields of research and teaching interests ran the gamut from the most ancient Indo-European languages to the most recent African American literature. In short, I will offer tentative explanations for the urgency of the topic to students, professors, and independent scholars who engage in philology, linguistics, literary history, literary criticism, and literary theory.

While describing and explaining the conference, I expect that the relevance of the topic to comparatists (and the appropriateness of the proceedings to *Comparative Literature Studies*) will become apparent.

Conservative-minded readers might feel that a collection of essays on the meaning of philology is innately comparative, since it looks to the roots from which the field of comparative literature has grown. Fans of literary theory will notice the prominent theorists on the roster of speakers and conclude that the conference had to have been comparative, because, rightly or wrongly, comparative literature and literary theory have become closely intertwined. Finally, even those who regard neither philology nor theory as being intrinsically comparatist will see that almost all of the essays do nothing if not compare—compare approaches to literature with each other, with approaches to other disciplines, or with social or political atmospheres. A few essays even compare literary texts.

*   *   *

Since the academic year 1986–87, the Center for Literary and Cultural Studies at Harvard University has sponsored an annual conference. In the fall of 1987 Marjorie Garber, the Director of the Center, convened a meeting at which Seminar Directors and members of the Executive Committee were asked to put forward suitable topics for the second annual conference. I proposed "What is Philology?," a question that had preoccupied me both as a Latinist and as a medievalist. Through my research in medieval Latin studies I had felt a steadily mounting awe at the methods that classical philologists have developed over the centuries, and at the value of the findings that they have reached. At the same time I had noticed that the mere utterance of the term *philology* in meetings of the Department of the Classics had a polarizing effect. Why would such an admirable array of techniques and knowledge inspire such fierce pride and protectiveness on one side and such deep-seated distrust and even resentment on the other?

But it was not because of Classics alone that I pondered philology. Among my fellow medievalists I had noticed an intensifying restiveness with philology in those fields, such as Romance philology, where the word is still frequently encountered. Sometimes philology is belittled as being a set of basic tools or data rather than as an approach valid in its own right. For instance, not long before the conference I read in a book on Old French literature: "Philology is the initiatory voyage of the medievalist, though to posit it as an autonomous branch of knowledge is to imagine the anthropologist who never returns to assess the meaning of his material."[1] This statement suggests the unfavorable contrast that is commonly drawn between the methods and models of philology and the social sciences. Philology is also presented unflatteringly as a phase in the growth of literary studies that has been almost superseded ("an aging Lady Philology").[2] According to this estimation, scholars in the philological period deluded themselves into believing that they were objective, whereas in fact they were motivated by an ideology that matched the colonialist and racist attitudes of the nineteenth century.[3]

In both Classics and medieval studies I sensed a sharp divide. At one extreme stand the self-proclaimed defenders of philology, who fear that extremely refined techniques acquired through centuries of learned enterprise run the danger of being spurned and lost. At the other are positioned those who worry that philologists have lost the ability or desire to test their own presuppositions and to ask new questions, and that consequently their areas of study have become stale and irrelevant. In between crouch the poor souls caught in the crossfire. They are likely to be considered too philological by certain of their colleagues and students, not philological enough by others. They may hedge their bets by continuing to read and sharpen their philological skills while waiting to see if any of the innovations will bring worthwhile rewards to their fields.

Where lies the truth—or where lie the truths—about philology? When drafting a brief written proposal I envisaged a conference at which faculty members from several departments could examine their conceptions of philology and engage in a philological analysis of philology. Matters to be considered included: the earliest uses and subsequent application of the word *philology* in various disciplines; the differences between philology and exegesis in the study of sacred texts; the relationship between philology and linguistics; and the place of philology in literary criticism.

At first the topic sounded peripheral to the interests of the members of the Steering Committee, most of whom work with modern literatures; for although the role of philology is often hotly debated by classicists and medievalists, the topic is seldom discussed by modernists. But I pressed the case that many scholars of ancient and medieval languages and literatures would be enthusiastic about coming to grips with the meaning and valuation of *philology;* and that whatever our chronological focus or theoretical banner, all of us live at least subliminally with philology, since we read and publish articles in journals that proclaim their allegiance in either their titles (such as *American Journal of Philology, Classical Philology, Harvard Studies in Classical Philology, Modern Philology, Neuphilologische*

Mitteilungen, Philological Quarterly, Philologus, Romance Philology, Zeitschrift für deutsche Philologie, and *Zeitschrift für romanische Philologie*) or their subtitles (such as *Anglia: Zeitschrift für englische Philologie, Eranos: Acta philologica Suecana, Hermes: Zeitschrift für klassische Philologie,* and *Wiener Studien: Zeitschrift für klassische Philologie und Patristik*).

None of my arguments moved anyone greatly. What most seized the imaginations of my colleagues and convinced them that the conference would have a broad appeal was being reminded of Paul de Man's essay entitled "The Return to Philology."[4] The apparent advocacy of a new and improved form of philology by one of the foremost literary theorists in America made the topic relevant to many who would otherwise have paid little attention to it; and local interest was heightened since de Man's essay was a riposte to an article by one of Harvard's best-known professors of English, Walter Jackson Bate.[5] A final spur to the excitement was the recollection that the current clash between philology and literary theory had been memorably anticipated in the nineteenth-century clash between Ulrich von Wilamowitz-Moellendorf and Friedrich Nietzsche.[6]

Once the notion of a conference on philology had been approved, the next stage was to set a roster of speakers and respondents. My original list of eleven possible discussants went through substantial changes at the hands of the "Philology Conference Committee" (Marjorie Garber, Barbara Johnson, John Koch, Gregory Nagy, and myself). For instance, members of the Committee were rightly troubled because the first list included only one woman. I had noticed this disproportion myself, but I had not devised a means of correcting it. Although the number of female professors at Harvard in language and literature departments has been increasing, most specialize in the Renaissance or later periods. In addition, most are literary critics, historians, or theorists. Few engage in research or teaching that is largely philological, as classicists or medievalists would define it. Indeed, Margaret Alexiou referred to this "gender gap" in her talk when she described philology in earlier times as "a male-dominated preserve." Nonetheless, through imaginative substitutions the roster of twelve speakers and respondents was broadened to include three women.

An equally major change was that proposed speakers who work with ancient or medieval languages and literatures, such as Assyrian and Old English, gave way to experts in more recent languages and literatures, such as Modern Greek and African American literature. Completing the mixture, one speaker and one respondent widely known as literary theorists earned niches on the list.

The final program comprised three sessions, each with three speakers and one respondent. I oversaw the opening session entitled "What is at Issue?" in which Wendell Clausen, Eckehard Simon, and Calvert Watkins spoke. Jonathan Culler served as respondent for the central session entitled "What is at Stake?" in which Barbara Johnson, John Koch, and Gregory Nagy delivered papers. Stephen Owen responded to the concluding round entitled "What Next?" in which Margaret Alexiou, Carolivia Herron, and Richard Thomas talked. To top off the day was an open discussion, under the heading "So What?"

*   *   *

At the conference one of the respondents, Jonathan Culler, asked me to enunciate my own view of philology. I demurred, confessing that I had organized the conference precisely because I wanted to find out what philology was. At this point I still lack the courage to offer a dictionary-style definition; but in conveying what I learned about philology from the conference, I will circumscribe the term as best I can. To do otherwise would be irresponsible, since in making the conference alluring and all-encompassing we risked stretching its meaning to the breaking point. How useful would the term *philology* (or *literary theory*, for that matter) be if it described any literary critical technique whatsoever?

The word *philology* has long led a confused existence in English. Consider the two main definitions in the original edition of the *Oxford English Dictionary*:

1. Love of learning and literature; the study of literature, in a wide sense, including grammar, literary criticism and interpretation, the relation of literature and written records to history, etc.; literary or classical scholarship; polite learning. Now *rare* in *general* sense.

3. *spec.* (in mod. use) The study of the structure and development of language; the science of language; linguistics (Really one branch of sense 1.)

The second edition of *Webster's New Universal Unabridged Dictionary* gives the appearance of greater clarity, but upon closer examination the appearance turns out to be a mirage:

1. originally, the love of learning and literature; study; scholarship.
2. the study of written records, especially literary texts, in order to determine their authenticity, meaning, etc.
3. linguistics: the current use.

At the conference the equation of philology with linguistics was rejected without any objections. Although the general sense of "love of learning and literature" was occasionally mentioned, most of the conference was spent in assessing the utility of philology in determining what *Webster's* so amusingly and evasively designated the "authenticity, meaning, etc." of written records.

If philology can be seen most broadly (and perhaps *too* broadly) as "the art of reading slowly," it is more narrowly a slow reading that aims at establishing and commenting upon documents.[7] As the Byzantinist Ihor Ševčenko once observed pithily in a departmental meaning, "Philology is constituting and interpreting the texts that have come down to us. It is a narrow thing, but without it nothing else is possible." This definition accords with Saussure's succinct description of the mission of philology: "especially to correct, interpret, and comment upon texts."[8]

What is it to constitute a text? Despite occasional reminders (such as the recent controversy over the text of Joyce's *Ulysses*), the difficulty and importance of establishing texts is sometimes forgotten by modernists. But scholars of earlier languages and literatures must confront the special demands of dealing with cuneiform tablets, papyri, and parchment, and the challenges of differentiating between scribal and authorial texts. Such scholars must employ methods such as paleography, codicology, and textual criticism. These methods seem to me constituents of philology, when it is broadly conceived.

Establishing a text is far from being a mechanical act. On the contrary, editing cannot proceed without interpretation and commentary. If editing is a philological activity, and if editing entails interpreting and commenting, is all interpretation and commentary intrinsically philological? Ay, there's the rub.

Let us look closely at a few forms of interpretation and commentary that are commonly held to be philological. One way of understanding a text is to look at the words individually and to determine their meanings on the basis of earlier and later evidence. But although *Wortphilologie* is one of philology's divisions, philology is not just a grand etymological or lexicographic enterprise. It also involves restoring to words as much of their original life and nuances as we can manage. To read the written records of bygone civilizations correctly requires knowledge of cultural history in a broad sense: of folklore, legends, laws, and customs. Philology also encompasses the forms in which texts express their messages, and thus it includes stylistics, metrics, and similar studies.

From the foregoing description it will be clear that the utility, applicability, and very meaning of philology will vary considerably from field to field. In fields in which the establishment of a text and its interpretation (either implicit or explicit) are inextricably intertwined, philology is often regarded as indispensable and held in high regard. In others many branches of philology will be needed less frequently.

There are other reasons for which the perception of philology will vary from one field to another. Here the differences between classical Greek and Latin literatures are instructive. To speak *grosso modo*, much of archaic Greek literature must be considered against the backdrop of an oral culture and ritual performance, whereas most classical Latin literature of the Golden and Silver Ages was produced by a highly literate culture and lacks a close connection with ritual. Consequently, the Latinist is likelier to devote his attention to approaches that emphasize comparing one work of literature with another, whereas the Hellenist will adapt methods from the social sciences to reconstruct ritual contexts. However different their perspectives and results, both sets of approaches must rely ultimately upon philological study of textual and lexical evidence as a means of interpreting literature.

Whatever the field, whether or not a person will want to study and apply philology depends somewhat upon disposition; for personality undoubtedly plays a part in the outlook that a person takes upon literature. Just as some people shrink from dealing with concepts and ideas, so others pull back from mustering knowledge and facts. Whereas some work from ideas back to the texts, others develop ideas through texts. To tamper with a phrase that is so popular in literary scholarship today, for everyone who resists theory, there is someone else who resists philology.[9]

* * *

At the conference much of the debate was concerned not with defining philology, but with determining its place in the hierarchy of literary

studies. Wendell Clausen, the first speaker, stated categorically that "philology is the basis of literary criticism." In contrast Jonathan Culler took
issue both with the particular idea of philology as basis, bedrock, and
foundation, and with the general notion of attempting to reconstruct
cultures and texts. Yet how are we to choose between the two possibilities
(philology as basis, philology not as basis) if we do not know what will
replace philology, so that we can weigh its advantages and disadvantages?
To speak of encountering "the other" in texts is exciting, but what are to
be the methods of "otherology" or "alteritics?"

According to an aphorism that dates to Hippocrates, a physician of the
fifth century B.C.: "Life is short, the skill time-consuming."[10] Although it
describes the demands of medicine, the aphorism sums up the situation of
most scholars in this busy world of ours. Our time is too short for us to
leave tried and true approaches and to risk unspecified innovations before
their applicability to our fields has been demonstrated. Indeed, classical
and medieval philologists have been strongly receptive to innovative
approaches, when the proponents of these approaches have taken the
time to apply them in interpreting texts from earlier cultures: one need
consider only the steady stream of interest in oral-formulaic literature
thanks to Milman Parry and Albert B. Lord, in structuralism thanks to
Georges Dumézil, or in reception-theory thanks to Hans Robert Jauss.

In my opinion the current controversy over the weight that should be
given to theory in the formation of literary scholars bears a striking resem-
blance to the impassioned twelfth-century debate on the curriculum and
syllabus, although in the twelfth century the governing terms were not
philology and theory, but grammar and dialectic, and the chief villain was
not Jacques Derrida, but Aristotle.[11] Under the old system, the methods
(*rationes*) of a given field were imparted through close work with standard
authors (*auctores*); under the new, through study of logical principles in
Aristotelian philosophy freshly translated from Greek and Arabic. People
(usually men!) who had received conventional training in *grammatica*
watched the flowering of dialectic distrustfully, believing that the new
discipline allowed intelligent youths to attain eminence in spite of their
ignorance. Such distrust will be awakened whenever a method that stresses
sheer logic competes with one that values the authority (*auctoritas*) of
accumulated learning.

Unless a balance is struck between the warring camps of our own day,
philology and theory could both go the way of grammar, dialectic, and

rhetoric: the once unchallenged *trivium* of verbal arts ended by becoming trivial. To reach a meaningful equilibrium, we must as a profession recognize the importance of both thinking about what we are doing and knowing what we are doing.

On the one hand, we must recognize that exposure to methodologies should not come at the expense of "hard skills." Sometimes I fear that in many areas of literary studies we have already reached the sad pass of producing students who are unable or unwilling to consult dictionaries and similar resources, even though the computer has made such consultation less time-consuming than ever before. No one would dispute that words are slippery things. At issue is whether we should make a cult of their slipperiness, or whether we should do the best we can to hold onto them and understand them. When faced with ambiguity, we can rank different interpretations on the basis of the probabilities as we see them. To do so should not mean that we claim infallibility, or that we cannot change our opinions after further reflection or after acquisition of further evidence.

On the other hand, philologists must realize that making their texts relevant to a modern audience, which necessitates asking new questions of their texts, is not inherently meretricious; on the contrary, it is an urgent desideratum. Most people are drawn to literature for pleasure and intellectual challenge (what was once called entertainment and edification), not for the satisfaction of exercising well-honed technical skills. Just as knowledge will be lost if old standards are dropped, so too fields will die if their representatives cannot find meaning for today's readers and today's new questions in the texts. At a time when literature in printed form has taken a back seat to television, film, and music, it is extremely important that scholars be able to articulate why students and colleagues should care about the books with which they work.

* * *

One surprise of the "What is Philology?" conference was the extent to which the debate over the place of philology in the curriculum was presented unabashedly as a power struggle. Indeed, philology seemed less at issue than philocracy when Gregory Nagy (in the oral form of his paper) declared: "here is what I think is really at stake: power, political power" and "the stakes involved, that is to say, the power I am looking for." [12] Jonathan Culler, who adverted briefly to the question of power, said that

what was at stake in the conference was the division of the kingdom of
P's, by which he referred to the language and literature call numbers in
the Library of Congress cataloging system. Margaret Alexiou spoke of a
struggle for hegemony, referring specifically to sexism and nationism in
the history of philological studies. Carolivia Herron described how she
unites pleasure and political activism in reading epics: in her words, she
draws philological interconnections between classical European and Afro-
American literature as a political method of gaining the attention of those
who hold the power of canonical reading lists in their hands.

Do philologists exert a stranglehold on power that justifies this rhetoric
of exclusion? Perhaps they still do so within a few departments, but not
within the University as a whole. At the Center for Literary and Cultural
Studies at Harvard Lady Theory is *prima inter pares*, since the Seminar on
Theory and Interpretation of Literature is given top billing in all the
brochures and schedules; "aging Lady Philology" is altogether absent from
the titles of the other seminars, which are arranged alphabetically. In the
"Literature and Arts A" division of the Core Curriculum (the division
with which I am most familiar) fifteen courses are listed, four by women
involved in this conference. Nowhere in the descriptions of these courses
does one's eye meet the word *philology*, whereas anthropological and psy-
choanalytic approaches are mentioned explicitly. Whether the rhetoric is
a cynical ploy or a remnant of bygone injustice, it has become anachronis-
tic. Philologists could make a strong case that lately they have been the
victims, not the perpetrators, of exclusion.

*   *   *

On the day of the conference I made every effort to be neutral, as
befitted my role as organizer and moderator; but in portraying the conference here I have not concealed my sympathies with the philologists. I owe
this allegiance partly to academic training, partly to family background,
and partly to temperament. Yet although my sympathies were with the
philologists, all the speakers at the conference were too intelligent and
honest in describing their attitudes toward philology and their passion for
literature for me not to have learned from them all. It was stirring to hear
colleagues distill the philosophy behind their life's work into talks of ten
or fifteen minutes.

The greatest virtue of the conference was in making a large group of

literary scholars realize that they have in common a love of literature and
close reading. Few of us believed that such love of learning and literature
by itself constitutes philology, although we have seen how the word had
that sense in the past. Few wished the word *philology* to become meaning-
lessly vague, both because philologists are jealous of their hard-won cre-
dentials and because many literary scholars of different stripes would not
wish to be considered philologists.

The conference also guided me to the conviction that we cannot allow
our profession to be split into two castes, one of which devotes itself
wholly to conceptual work, the other to textual or technical work. The
labor of erecting a building or bridge may be divided between an architect
who oversees the overall conception and a civil engineer who makes sure
that the resultant edifice does not collapse, but not so in literature! If all
of us love reading and agree with the old proverb that "to read and not to
understand is to disregard," then we should seek the middle ground.[13] But
is there a middle ground between the deconstructive aims of some theory
and the reconstructive project of all philology?

Harvard University

NOTES

1. R. Howard Bloch, *Etymologies and Genealogies: A Literary Anthropology of the French Middle Ages* (Chicago: U of Chicago P, 1983) 235, n.19.

2. María Rosa Menocal, *The Arabic Role in Medieval Literary History: A Forgotten Heritage* (Philadelphia: U of Pennsylvania P, 1987) ix.

3. Menocal, *The Arabic Role,* passim.

4. See Paul de Man, "The Return to Philology," in *The Resistance to Theory* (Minneapolis: U of Minnesota P, 1986) 21–26.

5. Walter Jackson Bate, "The Crisis in English Studies," *Harvard Magazine* (September–
October 1982): 46–53. During the conference more references were made to Bate's article
than to any other.

6. See "Nietzsche on Classics and Classicists (Part II)," selected and trans. William
Arrowsmith, *Arethusa* 2/3 (1963): 5–27, and Friedrich Nietzsche, *On the Future of Our
Educational Institutions: Homer and Classical Philology,* trans. J. M. Kennedy (New York:
Russell & Russell, 1964).

7. The quotation is of Roman Jakobson, from Calvert Watkins. At the conference the
quotation was repeated by both Barbara Johnson and Jonathan Culler.

8. Ferdinand de Saussure, *Course in General Linguistics*, ed. Charles Bally and Albert Sechehaye, in collaboration with Albert Riedlinger, trans. Wade Baskin (New York: McGraw-Hill, 1966) 1. I was led to this quotation by Calvert Watkins, who cites it in his paper.

9. The turn of phrase comes from Paul de Man, *The Resistance to Theory*.

10. "Vita brevis, ars longa": see August Otto, *Die Sprichwörter und sprichwörtlichen Redensarten der Römer* (Leipzig: B. G. Teubner, 1890) 375, no. 1915.

11. For a quick overview of the twelfth-century debate, see Jan Ziolkowski, *Alan of Lille's Grammar of Sex: The Meaning of Grammar to a Twelfth-Century Intellectual*, Speculum Anniversary Monographs 10 (Cambridge, Mass.: The Medieval Academy of America, 1985) 77–89 (especially 86–88).

12. Gregory Nagy notes that he was seeking to define power as an issue in the fifth century.

13. "legere enim et non intellegere neglegere est." The wordplay occurs in the prologue to the *Dicta Catonis*, ed. and trans. J. Wight Duff and Arnold M. Duff, *Minor Latin Poets*, Loeb Classical Library (Cambridge, Mass.: Harvard UP, 1934) 592. See Otto, *Die Sprichwörter*, 189, no. 928.

Philology

WENDELL CLAUSEN

Anyone who speaks about philology today must be aware that it has become, for many, a pejorative term, even a term of abuse; at the very least, an adverse relation seems to be implied: philology and . . . literary criticism or theory. Such a contrast—I am thinking especially, though not exclusively, of Greek and Latin literature—is not only futile, it is subversive; for philology is the basis of literary criticism. Too often philology has been humbled and identified with one or another of its components—with grammar (say) or textual criticism—and its original high purpose forgotten, which is, as it has been since the time of the scholars and poet-scholars of Alexandria, literary criticism—in Quintilian's phrase, *poetarum enarratio,* the detailed interpretation of the poets.

We are all of us natural philologists, growing up in our language, hearing, speaking, for the most part hardly even noticing it, so natural does it seem. But in Greek or Latin, in attempting to hear a "dead" language, we are deprived of the living voice; and it is the office of philology to supply our want of natural sensibility.

At the end of World War II, in 1945, a short book was published in Sweden, *Unpoetische Wörter* by Bertil Axelson, the importance of which, partly owing to circumstances, was only gradually recognized. Axelson undertook to answer an apparently simple question—in fact, a brilliant negative question: what words metrically available to the Latin poets did they avoid using? Unpoetic words: words unsuitable, presumably because of tone or connotation, to a certain genre of poetry, to poetry of a certain period, or altogether unsuitable. I remember still my surprise and dismay on first reading Axelson as a young scholar; for I was made to realize that I was not, after all, as I had fondly imagined, a Roman. The philologist, the classical scholar, must always be contemplating an imagined reality, an Italy of the mind, with the broken statues standing on the shore.

But to turn to a specific case, a *specimen criticum*, a question of hearing: you have before you the opening lines of a witty poem addressed by Catullus to his farm. Seeking a dinner invitation from a prominent politician named Sestius, Catullus had read one of his speeches. But its style was so "frigid" that Catullus caught a cold instead and retired to his farm to convalesce—his Tiburtine farm, as he maintains; as others maintain, his Sabine farm. Tibur (Tivoli) was a fashionable resort on the edge of the Sabine country; to a Roman the adjective *Sabinus* might suggest pristine Italic virtue or (as here) tedious and unrelieved rusticity.

> O funde noster, seu Sabine seu Tiburs
> (nam te esse Tiburtem autumant, quibus non est
> cordi Catullum laedere; at quibus cordi est,
> quouis Sabinum pignore esse contendunt),
> sed seu Sabine siue uerius Tiburs,
> fui libenter in tua suburbana
> uilla, malamque pectore expuli tussim.
>
> (44.1–7)

In my translation I have tried to represent the tone—as I hear it—and something of the meter: the choliambic or limping iambic, with a moment of arrest, a trochee in the final foot instead of an iamb:

> My dear farm, whether Sabine or Tiburtine
> (For those who do not like to hurt Catullus
> Say you are Tiburtine, but those who like to
> Will wager anything that you are Sabine),
> But whether Sabine or, in truth, Tiburtine,
> I had a pleasant stay in your suburban
> Villa, and cleared my chest there of a bad cough.

"O funde noster"—how is the vocative to be heard? What is its tone? Ellis, Baehrens, Friedrich, Kroll, and Fordyce—five important commentators—have nothing on "o funde noster"; an evasion of responsibility, for this form of the vocative is unique in Catullus and determines the tone of his poem. Quinn, whose commentary is now, I suppose, the most often used in courses, has only this tentative note: "The vocative personifies, and C.'s farm becomes the recipient of a verse epistle—perhaps even a divinity to whom C. can offer mock thanks for his cure (which would explain C.'s anxiety to ensure the farm is properly addressed)."[1] Quinn is partly right—the poem is an epistle, an urbane and wryly humorous thank-you note—and partly wrong: "o funde noster" is an elegant colloquialism, with no relation to sacral utterance. In Terence's *Adelphi* (883), Demea greets the slave Syrus with "o Syre noster, salue." But was this familiar form of address still current, a hundred years later, in Catullus' day? It was—or I would not be putting the question—as we can learn from Varro, a contemporary of Catullus. In his *Res Rusticae* Varro presents a small group of Roman gentlemen, close friends, talking about farming, and they address one another as "o Faustule noster" (2.3.1) (which the Loeb translator, quite rightly in my opinion, renders as "my dear Faustulus"), "o Merula noster," (3.14.1) "o Axi noster," (3.14.1) "o Pinni noster" (3.17.10)—"o funde noster" (it will be remembered that Catullus' farm had no agreed-upon name).

"O funde noster, seu Sabina seu Tiburs"—perhaps you can now hear something of the tone, the living voice.

Harvard University

NOTE

1. K. Quinn, *Catullus The Poems* (London, 1970) 221.

The Case for Medieval Philology

ECKEHARD SIMON

A century ago, Harvard established its Graduate School, or, more accurately, organized the Faculty of Arts and Sciences "to have charge," as President Charles W. Eliot wrote in the Report for 1889–90, "of the College, the Scientific School, and the Graduate School."[1] Next to Jewish Aramaic, Assyrian, and Old Iranian, an aspiring language student could, in that notable year, take Germanic Philology 1, Gothic, from Assistant Professor (of Romance languages, no less!) Sheldon, German Philology 2, Old High German and Old Saxon, from Assistant Professor von Jagemann, and Germanic Philology 3, Old Norse, with "Mr. Kittredge."[2] We all know that Mr. Kittredge had a bright future. But it marked the rise of Germanic Philology that the Old High German instructor, Hans Carl Günter von Jagemann, was appointed Harvard's first Professor of Germanic Philology in 1898. Germanic philology was being established, at Harvard and other American Graduate Schools, on the model of the highly respected German, notably Prussian, university curriculum. In fact, the Graduate School had itself been created in the German image and as early as 1880 the Faculty had awarded a Ph.D. in Germanic philology ("The Language of the Ormulum and Its Relations with Old English").

Few of us remember today how influential the German tradition was in America before World War I. In our schools, German was the most popular foreign language. In 1903, Kuno Francke, Professor of the History of German Culture, founded Harvard's "Germanic Museum" to rival such eminent local institutes as the Peabody Museum of Ethnology and the Semitic Museum. In June of 1909, Schiller's "Die Jungfrau von Orleans" was performed, as class play, before the university's students and professors in Harvard Stadium, with a setting reminiscent of a medieval Passion Play.

When the department of Germanic Languages and Literatures began to train its own doctoral students, many chose to write dissertations on formidable philological topics such as "The Use of the Infinitive in Berthold von Regensburg" (1896) or "Studies in the Syntax and Style of Meister Eckhart" (1899). Although it took until 1922 before a Radcliffe woman earned a Ph.D. in Germanic, her dissertation was, again, in philology ("Eine Darstellung der Lautlehre des Hans Sachs, wie sie in seinen Handschriften erscheint").

By that time, philology of the Germanic kind was an ubiquitous muse and, with textbooks published in Leipzig and Tübingen, had taken over the English department. In fact, Professor W. Jackson Bate, in a spirited 1982 review of English studies, claims that "philology"—or "the study of words historically," as he defines it—"achieved a stranglehold on English studies from the 1880s to the 1940s."[3] Perhaps recalling the more unpleasant of his graduate school days, Professor Bate draws a remarkable picture of English in the chains of philology:

> If you took a Ph.D. here in English as late as the 1930s, you were suddenly shoved—with grammars written in German—into Anglo-Saxon, and Middle Scots, *plus* Old Norse (Icelandic), Gothic, Old French, and so on. I used to sympathize with the Japanese and Chinese students who had come here to study literature struggling with a German grammar to translate Gothic into English! William Allan Neilson, the famous president of Smith College, had been a professor of English here for years. Forgiveably, he stated that the Egyptians took only five weeks to make a mummy, but the Harvard English Department took five years.[4]

Among graduate students, regimentation of this sort produced a syndrome known as "philology anxiety," a dread affliction that as late as the sixties prompted a colleague of mine, now a distinguished literary theorist, to write Gothic conjugations on her bed sheet.

The Harvard English department, we note with gratitude, did not succeed in mummifying all of its graduate students. And at least two of them, Professor Bate himself and Harry Levin, would soon see to it that things were changed. By the fifties, philology was everywhere in retreat before the paperback-flinging troops of the New Criticism.

But what Professor Bate witnessed was, I submit, the gradual perversion of a discipline in the hands of marginal minds who must have been unforgiveably bad teachers. Philology does not mean "open your Gothic grammar and translate." The founders of Germanic philology, Jacob and Wilhelm Grimm, Georg Friedrich Benecke, and Karl Lachmann, would not have agreed with Bate's definition of philology as "the study of words historically." For Jacob Grimm, the philologist's task was to study the entire written record of the past, from runic inscriptions and law codes to folk tales and "Poesie" or literature, and apply to it, as we would say, a vast amount of interdisciplinary knowledge.[5] "Der Zweck der Philologie," as Friedrich Schlegel put it most succinctly, "ist die Historie."[6] Schlegel and Grimm, then, saw philology as having the capacity to retrieve the experiences of the past, of lost cultures, through close study of the written record. The only discipline where "Philologie" so defined is still being practiced today is "Klassische Philologie," that is, classical studies.

The burden of past scholarship may weigh too heavily on us ever to return to Schlegel's "Philologie als Kulturwissenschaft," as the concept was recently formulated to honor Germany's most eminent practitioner of Germanic philology.[7] But what we do in medieval studies has, in recent years, begun to resemble the work of our brethren in classical studies, who still conceive of their field as an entity and where a literary historian will also know something about paleography, coins, or pottery shards. Medieval studies stands much to gain from building itself in the image of classical studies.

Given the overwhelming importance of the written record, medieval studies so defined should also prompt us to liberate Lady Philology from the academic attic to which misguided followers had her consigned. For basic to medieval studies must be a command of medieval languages. The growing reliance on translations is a threat to authoritative scholarship. A scholar must be able to check out textual evidence in the original source, whether this be a literary manuscript, a charter, or an account roll.

In my own field of medieval German, it is now especially important to return to a rigorous pursuit of philology in its original meaning, that is, the study of the written record in its cultural context. We have learned by now that the Middle High German of our editions was never written by any poet and—in Lachmann's standardized form—was never heard by a medieval audience. What authors used were modified versions of their regional dialects, about what we find in the older manuscripts. In fact, we are no longer certain that the modern idea of an "original text" (the infamous "archetype") was an operative concept among medieval poets. The *Nibelungenlied* is now being read in three versions. And while B may indeed have been the first, it was only a matter of years before two equally anonymous "redactors," tapping living oral narrative, produced a longer (C) and a shorter text (A). Lyric poets appear to have sung, over time, new versions of old songs, perhaps to suit different courts. And the minstrel generations to come continued this practice with wild copyright abandon, so that virtually every manuscript we have contains a different text of the same song.

What all this suggests is that we will soon be reading the manuscripts themselves, which will require a good deal of hard practice and patient learning. Students will have to develop the ability to transcribe and edit their own texts, thus restoring respect for the demanding and honorable craft of editing that is basic to all we do. The codices themselves will be studied as depositories of cultural history. Here, then, is our case for medieval philology. It calls for a return to hands-on philology of the old kind which, while challenging and requiring sustained effort, should also be more fun than translating Gothic: reading texts in all kinds of manuscripts (that is, in the many excellent facsimiles now available), becoming conversant with the history of time and place, discovering medieval culture, as Jacob Grimm might have put it, through informed study of the written record.

Harvard University

NOTES

1. *Annual Report of the President and Treasurer of Harvard College, 1889–90* (Cambridge, Mass.: The University, 1891) 4.

2. *Report,* 72.

3. W. Jackson Bate, "The Crisis in English Studies," *Harvard Magazine* (September–October 1982): 46–53, here 49.

4. Bate 49.

5. For a revisionist reading, see Ulrich Wyss, *Die wilde Philologie, Jacob Grimm und der Historismus* (Munich: C. H. Beck, 1979).

6. Friedrich Schlegel, "Philosophie der Philologie," cited from Karl Stackmann, "Die Klassische Philologie und die Anfänge der Germanistik," in *Philologie und Hermeneutik im 19. Jahrhundert. Zur Geschichte und Methodologie der Geisteswissenschaften*, ed. Hellmut Flashar *et al.* (Göttingen: Vandenhoeck & Ruprecht, 1979) 240–59, here 258.

7. *Philologie als Kulturwissenschaft: Studien zur Literatur und Geschichte des Mittelalters. Festschrift für Karl Stackmann zum 65. Geburtstag*, ed. Ludger Grenzmann *et al.* (Göttingen: Vandenhoeck & Ruprecht, 1987).

What is Philology?

CALVERT WATKINS

Some thirty-three years ago, when I was being interviewed as a candidate for Harvard's Society of Fellows, I was asked what I felt was the relation between linguistics and philology. I have no recollection of what I answered, but I do remember the historian Crane Brinton's response:

> It seems to come down to the question of which is the handmaiden of which?

The question before us is, what is philology? My answer will be to try and define it philologically, by looking at texts, in other words by doing philology.

Linguists in the past have sometimes been rather short with philology. Ferdinand de Saussure in the posthumous *Cours,* in his thumbnail sketch of the history of linguistics, gives the following 'second stage':

> Then came philology. . . . Language is not the unique object of philology. The task of philology is above all to establish, interpret, and comment upon texts. This just concern leads philology to concern itself with literary history, customs, institutions, etc. . . . Everywhere it makes use of its own method, which is textual criticism. But philology is deficient in one point: it is too slavishly attached to the written word and forgets spoken language; and

besides it is almost exclusively concerned with Greek and Latin antiquity."[1]

Now the claim that philology is "almost exclusively concerned with Greek and Latin antiquity" is of course nonsense, as the Germanists, Celticists, Hittitologists, Iranists, and Indologists among us would immediately agree. (I mention those just because they are the philologies I have to deal with every day.) Considerations of philology tend for historical reasons to begin with classical antiquity, and the Latinists begin and end this conference in good ring-composition style. But philology may be better integrated elsewhere, and a field where philology is more a standard tool than a separate and sometimes hostile discipline might be a good place to start to look at what philology is. It is perhaps true that there is more of a barrier between philology qua textual criticism, and linguistics or history or archaeology in the Classics than in some others: in Old Irish, or Hittite, or Vedic Sanskrit, or Indo-European studies, everyone does both linguistics and philology on a daily basis, and it's no big deal.

Saussure was at some pains to point out that the objects of linguistics and of philology were only coincidentally the same; saying in the third series of lectures in 1910–11,

> Most linguists do philology, which does not prevent the object *language* from remaining separate in principle from the textual material.[2]

Saussure's pupil Antoine Meillet in his wonderful little book of 1925 on *The Comparative Method in Historical Linguistics* is more stringent:

> To determine linguistic states of the past, the linguist must employ the most exact and the most precise philology. Every advance in philological precision permits new progress for the linguist. . . . But by itself philology cannot bring even a beginning of linguistic history.[3]

And Leonard Bloomfield a decade later also keeps the two firmly apart, but with an interesting definition of our word:

The term *philology,* in British and older American usage, is applied not only to the study of culture (especially through literary documents), but also to linguistics. It is important to distinguish between *philology* . . . and *linguistics* . . . , since the two studies have little in common.[4]

If philology is the study of culture (especially through literary documents) then philology would seem to be a branch of anthropology. This probably sits uncomfortably with my classical colleagues, but it is by no means absurd: Saussure in a letter to Meillet of January 4, 1894 wrote poignantly,

> In the last analysis it is only the picturesque side of a language, that which makes it differ from all others as belonging to a certain people having certain origins, it is this almost ethnographic side, which keeps its interest for me.[5]

What Saussure meant was precisely philology, as Jonathan Culler saw in his translation of the letter, when he interprets and translates a later passage as "spoil my pleasure in philology."[6] But note that for Saussere philology is not just texts, but "a certain people having certain origins."

It is sometimes instructive to observe one's own linguistic usage. I can recall having used the word philology only a couple of times in print. One was a paper given in Geneva a decade ago on Saussure's method, in which I tried

> to leave the floor to Saussure, to confront certain passages with certain others, and if I may call it that, to do Saussurian philology.[7]

In another (written in 1981) I ventured to suggest that

> . . . the historical linguist's first task is the interpretation of the meaning of a text. Now there is a realm of meaning called 'semantics', and a realm of meaning nowadays called 'pragmatics'. The latter . . . 'is the study of the meaning of language forms as these depend on the linkage of signs to the context in which they occur (we call this the "indexical" meaning of signs)' [Silverstein]. . . . Despite the relative novelty of isolating what it denotes—the his-

torical linguist has been dealing with this all along; he just calls it philology.[8]

Philology is also "the meaning of language forms as these depend on the linkage of signs to the context in which they occur."

Comparative Philology used to be a catch-all term for Linguistics, as it was formerly at Harvard. The change of name to Department of Linguistics in the late 40s was entirely appropriate, and indeed long overdue: comparative philology conceived as such had nothing to do with the object we are here to study. But that doesn't mean that there isn't something we can term the "new comparative philology" or the new comparative poetics and comparative ethnosemantics of Émile Benveniste.[9] This is for me—as it was for Saussure—the most pleasurable part of comparative linguistics. Let me just try and give a little illustration of what this comparative philology is, show how we use both linguistic and philological arguments, and show which is which.

I can state that Greek *ēthos* "custom, usage; abode; character" is related to Vedic *svadhā-* "self-power; own state, customary state; custom; abode," and to Latin *sod-alis* "(fellow) member of a paternity" and to the family of German *Sitte* "custom." The cognate set is reconstructible as *swe-dh(e)h-*. These are linguistic statements, which can be supported by linguistic arguments.

I can also state that the respectful term of address *ētheîos* (*ēthaîos*) in Greek, "trusty, customary, friend," is a derivative of *ēthos* "custom," just as Latin *sod-alis* is a derivation of *s(u)od-*. I can further assert that the term *ētheîos* pragmatically makes reference to, it *indexes* the inherited consecrated usage of the reciprocal gift-exchange relation (Greek *xenía*) between, e.g.,

That is to say, the meaning of *ētheîos* cannot be determined without indexical reference to this relation. In support I can adduce Pindar's referring to a patron in Isthmian 2.48 (470 B.C.?) as *xeînon emòn ēthaîon*, translating pregnantly "my 'customary' guest-friend" ("customary" in the sense "with whom one shares consecrated usage"). I can then compare our oldest attestation of the Latin cognate of *ēthaîos*, namely, *s(u)odalis* in a recently discovered archaic inscription, the lapis Satricanus (ca. 500 B.C.), perhaps the oldest text we have in the Latin language:

POPLIOSIO VALESIOSIO SVODALES

with again a pregnant translation "customary clients of Publius Valerius." Here I am making a linguistic (and ethnosemantic) statement, supported by philological arguments; and the comparison may also contribute to the interpretation of both passages, which is a philological goal.

Such are les plaisirs du texte.

What, then, is philology? Let me conclude with the definition of philology that my teacher Roman Jakobson gave (who got it from his teacher, who got it from his): "Philology is the art of reading slowly."

Harvard University

NOTES

1. Ferdinand de Saussure, *Cours de linguistique générale,* 2nd ed. (Paris: Payot, 1922) 13–4. (All translation is my own.)

2. Ferdinand de Saussure, *Cours de linguistique: édition critique,* ed. Rudolf Engler (Wiesbaden: Otto Harassowitz, 1967) 3:137.

3. Antoine Meillet, *La Méthode comparative en linguistique historique* (Oslo: H. Aschehoug & Co., 1925) 11.

4. Leonard Bloomfield, *Language* (New York: Holt, Rinehart and Winston, 1933) 512.

5. Ferdinand de Saussure, letter to Antoine Meillett, 4 January 1894, *Cahiers Ferdinand de Saussure* 21 (1964): 93–96.

6. Jonathan Culler, *Ferdinand de Saussure,* (New York: Penguin Books, 1977) 4.

7. Calvert Watkins, "Remarques sur la méthode de Ferdinand de Saussure comparatiste," *Cahiers Ferdinand de Saussure* 32 (1978): 59–69.

8. Calvert Watkins, "Language, culture, or history?" *Papers from the Parasession on Language and Behavior,* eds. Carrie S. Masek et al. (Chicago: Chicago Linguistic Society, U of Chicago, 1981) 238–48.

9. Émile Benveniste, *Le vocabulaire des institutions indo-européennes* (Paris: Les Éditions de Minuit, 1969). Note also: Calvert Watkins, "New Parameters in Historical Linguistics, Philology and Culture History," Presidential address to Linguistic Society of America, *Language* 65 (1989), forthcoming; "Questions linguistiques de poétique, de mythologie et de prédroit en indo-européen," *Lalies* 5 (1987): 3–29; "How to kill a dragon in Indo-European," *Studies in Memory of Warren Cowgill (1929–1985),* ed. Calvert Watkins (Berlin: de Gruyter, 1987) 270–99; "Aspects of Indo-European poetics," *The Indo-Europeans in the Fourth and Third Millennia,* ed. Edgar Polomé (Ann Arbor: Karoma, 1982) 104–20.

Philology: What is at Stake?

BARBARA JOHNSON

In an attempt to clarify what is at stake in the debates about the role of philology in literary studies, I will begin by turning to two polemical essays, one by William Arrowsmith, the other by Paul de Man; one an attack on philology, the other a plea for a return to philology. I will then illustrate each theoretical position by turning to a literary text.

Arrowsmith formulates his attack on philologists in the course of a presentation of Nietzsche's writings on classics and classicists. It is often forgotten that Nietzsche began as a classicist and a philologist—and this is indeed the side of Nietzsche with which de Man will claim affinity in his essay. Arrowsmith's most polemical remarks are made in the course of a discussion of Wilamowitz's attack on Nietzsche's book *The Birth of Tragedy from the Spirit of Music:*

> Classicists, of course, have unanimously preferred to believe that Wilamowitz—who caught Nietzsche in several factual errors—had the best of it. But in point of fact none of Wilamowitz's arguments disproves or even seriously damages Nietzsche's thesis; for the notion, particularly dear to philologists, that a thesis . . . is only as good as its author's philological expertise is clearly a fallacy. For although a sorites of rigorous argument and proofs may be relevant to strict philological work (such as the dating of a play), a thesis

like Nietzsche's—a large, intuitive, esthetic insight, addressed finally to esthetic experience—cannot be defeated by showing errors of fact in the argument. And to think that it could be is the kind of crude category-mistake to which philologists, insofar as they are primarily technicians, are professionally susceptible. But the consequence of this naive faith is, for classical studies, unfortunate. Not only is method pressed to the point where it finally begins to defeat thoughts and complexity, but the philologist, by dismissing literary insight as methodologically unsound, cuts himself off from the completion of his own purpose and skills. For supposedly philology aims at literary understanding.[1]

In a footnote, Arrowsmith pursues the conflict between aesthetic intuition and mere accuracy in the domain of literary translation:

There are, after all, more important things than accuracy—there is life, for instance. Only philologists could have built their distinctive professional virtue—accuracy—into a theory of translation. And the philological view of translation has lasted, not because it is commonsensical, but because philologists have appointed themselves the policemen of their own theory. In an age of specialization, the specialist usually frightens off the amateurs. But this triumph of professionalism is not necessarily a triumph of intelligence or truth.

This opposition between accuracy and truth, between the amateur and the police, can be seen to underlie the plot of Edgar Allan Poe's short story, "The Purloined Letter." The police, who are proud of the rigor of their professionalism, have searched every hidden inch of the minister's apartment without finding the letter the minister has stolen from the queen. An amateur detective, Auguste Dupin, is called in and, in one glance, he finds the letter hanging in plain sight. Jacques Lacan, in his analysis of "The Purloined Letter," uses terms very similar to Arrowsmith's to describe the small-mindedness of the police in contrast to the intuitive leap of Dupin. Dupin recognizes that the letter's position is a function of the repetitive logic of crime rather than a physical concealment in space. "A transition is made here," writes Lacan, "from the domain of exactitude to the register of truth."[2] Thus, Lacan's opposition between exactitude and truth very much echoes the terms of Arrowsmith's critique of philology.

This way of formulating the case against philology seems to me totally compelling. But exactitude may not be something so easily dismissed or taken for granted. As long as exactitude is subject to commonsensical norms of meaningfulness, as in the police's belief that what is not found must be hidden, Arrowsmith's and Lacan's critique of it seems irreproachable. But what if the close attention to the language of a text *didn't* produce a sensible or determinable meaning? What if the philologist's attentiveness to language were great enough to open up irresolvable difficulties, *resistances* to meaning, or other, unexpected meanings within the text? These are the questions Paul de Man raises in response to something like Arrowsmith's aesthetic intuitionism. In his essay entitled "The Return to Philology," de Man describes a course (affectionately known as Hum 6) taught at Harvard in the 1950s by Reuben Brower—a course that had a formative impact on de Man's own theories of reading. Here is de Man's description of the papers assigned for that course:

> Students, as they began to write on the writings of others, were not to say anything that was not derived from the text they were considering. They were not to make any statements that they could not support by a specific use of language that actually occurred in the text. They were asked, in other words, to begin by reading texts closely as texts and not to move at once into the general context of human experience or history. Much more humbly or modestly, they were to start out from the bafflement that such singular turns of tone, phrase, and figure were bound to produce in readers attentive enough not to hide their non-understanding behind the screen of received ideas that often passes, in literary instruction, for humanistic knowledge. . . . Mere reading, it turns out, prior to any theory, is able to transform critical discourse in a manner that would appear deeply subversive to those who think of the teaching of literature as a substitute for the teaching of theology, ethics, psychology, or intellectual history. Close reading accomplishes this often in spite of itself because it cannot fail to respond to structures of language which it is the more or less secret aim of literary teaching to keep hidden. . . .

The personal experience of Reuben Brower's Hum 6 was not so different from the impact of theory on the teaching of literature over the past ten or fifteen years. The motives may have been more revolutionary and the terminology was certainly more intimidating. But, in practice, the turn to theory occurred as a return to philology, to an examination of the structure of language prior to the meaning it produces.[3]

Interestingly enough, then, in view of the fact that recent polemics tend to oppose theory and philology, de Man is claiming here that what is truly radical in theory *is* philology.

To illustrate the utility of philology in this sense, I turn to another literary representation of a letter—the ransom note Bigger Thomas sends to his employer Mr. Dalton in Richard Wright's *Native Son*. Bigger has accidentally killed Dalton's daughter and wants to throw the blame on Communists. He therefore signs the letter "Red." The ransom note begins, "We got your daughter. She is safe." It continues with instructions about exchanging money for the daughter's return and ends, "When you see a light in a window blink three times, throw the box in the snow, and drive off. Do what this letter say."[4] Because the note is signed "Red," no one suspects Bigger of being the author. The police, again, are blinded by a preconception. It would take precisely a philologist to read the letter correctly and detect its authorship: the sentence "Do what this letter say" is a sign that the author is black, not red. Reading through *expectation* ("the screen of received ideas")—rather than through an encounter with the text's language—leads to blindness.

What is at stake, then, is clearly the nature of reading; the question is not whether to be or not to be philological but how to read in such a way as to break through preconceived notions of meaning in order to encounter unexpected otherness—in order to learn something one doesn't already know—in order to encounter the other. It is not easy to respond when literature tells us "Do what this letter say." To know whether this requires more closeness or more distance, a leap or a crawl, may very well *itself* be part of the challenge. For it is the question of the nature of the act of reading that philology can either illuminate or repress.

Harvard University

NOTES

1. William Arrowsmith, "Nietzsche on Classics and Classicists (Part II)," *Arethusa* 2 (1963): 8–10.

2. Jacques Lacan, "Seminar on 'The Purloined Letter,' " in *The Purloined Poe,* ed. John P. Muller and William J. Richardson (Baltimore: The Johns Hopkins UP, 1988) 35.

3. Paul de Man, *The Resistance to Theory* (Minneapolis: U of Minnesota P, 1986) 23, 24.

4. Richard Wright, *Native Son* (New York: Harper & Row, 1940) 166–67.

Thoughts on Celtic Philology and Philologists

JOHN T. KOCH

CELTIC Studies have a rich and enduring philological tradition. The historical and comparative study of language is primary, leading to the analysis of the texts embodying that language. The earlier periods have received the greatest attention, and the notion of Indo-European has loomed large.

I expect that this has not differed drastically from philology in other fields. So what I propose to talk about is not Celtic Philology *per se*, but rather some of its wider implications, which I hope might reflect on the broader issues of the formal study of minority languages and literatures. I will take up three themes: the minority philologist as Horatio Alger in the majority culture, minority philologist as cultural hero to the minority, and finally Celtic scholars' ambivalence towards the philological legacy. I should first point out that the status of the Celts as subjugated minorities in the English-speaking world is absolutely fundamental. Celtic had first to give ground before England and the English language could come into being. As we read in traditional history, the Celtic natives were either massacred by the invading Saxons or driven to the inhospitable mountain fastnesses and seagirt, windswept promontories of the far west.

I have more than once been reminded of this gripping scenario when passing through a place in Mid Wales called Ponterwyd, which happens to have been the home of my Horatio Alger, Sir John Rhŷs. Even in the context of the rugged and starkly beautiful region, the Ponterwyd neighbourhood stands out as rather god-forsaken. Rhŷs was the son of a farm labourer and sometime lead miner. He himself left the mines at 19, walking most of the hundred miles to teacher's college, "the Normal" in Bangor. While toiling away at his one-room schoolhouse in North Wales, Rhŷs taught himself Latin, Greek, French, and German. In 1865, he published "The Passive Verbs of the Latin and Celtic Languages" in the *Transactions of the Philological Society*, which deployed Welsh and Irish evidence to refute Bopp's then prevailing view that *rs* of the Latin passive endings had derived from earlier *ss* by rhotacism. That article brought him to the attention of Matthew Arnold and the Principal of Jesus College. Over the coming years, these two provided Rhŷs with grants and stipendiary appointments enabling him to study comparative philology in Paris, Heidelberg, Göttingen, and Leipzig and to obtain an Oxford BA. In 1877 he published his *Lectures on Welsh Philology*, which was, in his words, the first "systematic application of the comparative method" to his native language (v). In the same year, he was appointed as the first Professor of Celtic at Oxford (Foster 10–12; Morris-Jones 3–5; Parry-Williams 6–45). Some years before, the founding of the chair had been urged by Arnold and the Principal of Jesus in the name of the "Philologists of Germany" and the the "first occupants of this island," in that order of precedence (Foster 10). Rhŷs went on to publish extensively in Celtic philology, both *Sprach-* and *Literatur-wissenschaft*—mythology, ethnology, etc.—but what is of more importance for my present theme is that he ended his career as Principal of Jesus College, a Knight of the Privy Council, and with enough of a personal fortune that large grants are still made in his name to bring Celtic scholars to Oxford (Foster 12–14; Morris-Jones 9–28).

The function of philology in Rhŷs's success was as the science which afforded incontrovertible proof that the highly prestigious Greek and Latin, and the newcomer Sanskrit, were made of the very same stuff as his despised native language; likewise, that the overlooked Celtic literature could and should stand shoulder to shoulder with the canonised monuments of the mainstream of Western civilization. With the secret weapon of philology, Rhŷs shattered the persistent prejudice that minority ethnicity must be shed to "get on" in the greater world.

For the theme of the culture hero, I turn first to Nietzsche, who, in writing about his first profession as a classical philologist, likened his

colleagues to moles with full cheek pouches and blind eyes gleefully captur-
ing worms (Arrowsmith 7). Elsewhere, he wrote of dwarves in danger of
being crushed as they attempted to resurrect the colossus of classical
antiquity (Arrowsmith 7). In the little worlds of the Celtic countries, the
philologist's stature is neither dwarfish nor mole-like. My chosen exem-
plum is Rhŷs's greatest pupil, John Morris-Jones of Llanfairpwllgwyngyll-
gogerychwyrndrobwllllantysiliogogogoch in Anglesey. A complete renaissance man, he took his first degree in mathematics, invented electric
clocks, and not only designed the ornate seal of the University of Wales
Press, but carved the original die (Parry 6–9; Williams 17–72). As well as
being the author of the *Welsh Grammar, Historical and Comparative,* of
1913—not yet superseded and still cherished in Wales as a milestone of
nationhood—, he authoritatively edited and translated some of the earliest Welsh poetry, reformed the spelling of Modern Welsh—establishing
the orthography that remains standard today—, codified the principles of
the strict metres of traditional poetry, and was himself a major poet who
broke free from the artificial diction, forced allegory, and sentimentality
of the prevailing hymnological bards. For more than twenty years he
adjudicated the bardic chair at the National Eisteddfod. Virtually single-
handedly, it was Sir John—*he* also got knighthood for lifelong service to
Welsh philology—who ensured that Modern Welsh should have something that is very rare in a minority language, namely a literary standard
that is at once prestigious, widely known, and founded on sound historical
principles (Parry 27–59).

Within the smaller compass of the minority language the distance is
reduced from the ancient forms of the old manuscripts and inscriptions
to colloquial speech or contemporary literature. Here the "love of discourse" is less open to the charge of linguistic taxidermy or literary
necrophilia. In Welsh, e.g., *yr heniaith* "the ancient language" can refer
to the Old Welsh of the epics and inscriptions, but also means today's
Welsh, which is old in the sense of the mother tongue that preceded
English. There is a poem called "Heniaith" by the twentieth-century
bard Waldo Williams, where he says: *Nyni a wêl ei hurddas trwy niwl ei
hadfyd | codwn yma ei hen feini annistryw!* (1962) "We who see her
majesty through the fog of her degradation, come, let us raise here her
ancient stones undestroyed!" Not the appeal of necrophiliac dwarf; he is
talking about living Welsh. But in this metaphor the objective of the

philologist, the language movement, and even minority nationalism are one and the same—the strength and vision to restore a ruin, not as a museum piece, but as a functioning architecture. This metaphor was earlier used memorably by Matthew Arnold in his lectures *On the Study of Celtic Literature* in describing what is generally regarded as the greatest monument of early Welsh prose, the Mabinogion.

> The very first thing that strikes one, in reading the "Mabinogion", is how evidently the mediaeval story-teller is pillaging an antiquity of which he does not fully possess the secret; he is like a peasant building his hut on the site of Halicarnassus or Ephesus; he builds, but what he builds is full of materials of which he knows not the history, or knows by a glimmering tradition merely—stones "not of this building", but of an older architecture, greater, cunninger, more majestical. (46–47)

In turning to my final theme, I note again the pivotal role of the Philologists of Germany in the rise of Rhŷs, Morris-Jones, and other native scholars. Many of these foreigners spent much of their careers working directly with Celtic, scholars like Zeuss, Zimmer, Windisch, Kuno Meyer, Thurneysen (who was actually Swiss), Pedersen (a Dane), and Pokorny (Thurneysen 22–30). Meyer and Pokorny brought such passion to their work and spent so much time in Ireland that they became minor national heroes whose authority extended beyond academia (Meid; Watkins). However, it was inevitable that continental philology, rooted as it was in Indo-European and classicism, and native scholarship, tied as it was to the struggling dialects and patriotism, would have interests that would not always coincide.

Celtic scholarship has always been at pains to justify its existence in, for example, universities like Oxford, and Harvard and even to the Celts themselves with their ingrained sense of cultural inferiority and irrelevance. Philology has always been a part of that justification, but this use has involved a fallacy that may be termed *the prestige game*. That the Celtic langauges are closely related to Greek, Latin, and Sanskrit and reflect importantly upon the parent Indo-European is an objective, scientific fact. But that Greek, Latin, and Sanskrit have great prestige in academia and that Celtic can lay claim to a portion of that prestige is wholly subjective and is readily extended into sheer silliness. Old Irish, which has the oldest copious corpus of texts and preserves Indo-European archaisms lost in other stages and sister languages, holds highest prestige as the "Sanskrit of Celtic" (not my coining). Welsh, later Irish, etc., are accordingly lower in status. I have heard younger scholars in Ireland disparage an implicit and entrenched attitude that seventh-century texts were morally better than eighth-century texts. More than the foreign philologists, the misdirected *pietas* of their Irish pupils has been to blame here. At the low end of the hierarchy, the mystique of archaism has even led to a disdain for the beleaguered living languages which is joltingly reminiscent of the old colonial views.

Morris-Jones simply could not accept that Irish was better than Welsh as a reflection of "Proto-Keltic" and "Aryan." His grammar was seriously flawed by such biases. With Ireland the chief focus of attention for the foreign philologist, subsequent generations of Welsh scholars have tended to see Indo-European and Celtic Studies as of secondary importance at best, somebody else's rigged game at worst.

On both sides of the Irish Sea, the whole efficacy of a unified, philologically-defined Celtic Studies is openly questioned. To what extent can the notion of "the Celtic" be validly extended beyond the Indo-European family tree? How meaningful is this concept—as opposed to a separate Irish, Welsh, etc.— when we talk about Celtic literature, Celtic culture, Celtic history? Is Celtic an arbitrary shotgun wedding between nations profoundly different from, and ambivalent about, one another? For an analog, does the family-tree theory of linguistic evolution oblige the Lithuanian scholar to think Balto-Slavicly?

I for one defend the validity of unified Celtic Studies and philology's primacy therein. We must never take for granted where our languages came from or what our texts do and do not say. The future, though, will have to see the dismantling of the unscientific morality of archaism, which—incapable of an argued defense—has generated impediments and ill will through repeated insinuation and florid pronouncements. Celtic Studies can no longer take its angelic revenge upon the Philistines (Arnold's diction [137]) armed with an arrogance borrowed from nineteenth-century classicism. It must instead defend itself on its own terms, which may mean setting the first inhabitants of the British Isles ahead of the philologists of Germany.

Harvard University

WORKS CITED

Arnold, Matthew. *On the Study of Celtic Literature.* 1867. London, 1893.

Arrowsmith, William. "Nietzsche on Classics and Classicists (Part II)." *Arethusa* 2 (1963): 5–27.

Foster, Idris Ll. "Sir John Rhŷs." *Proceedings of the Seventh International Congress of Celtic Studies, Oxford, 1983.* Ed. D. Ellis Evans, John G. Gruffydd, and E. M. Jope. Oxford: D. Ellis Evans, 1986.

Gaidoz, H. "Deux érudits gallois: John Rhys et Llywarch Reynolds." *Revue Internationale de l'Enseignement,* 15 janvier–15 février 1916: 12–21, 104–14, 193–213, 274–85, 375–82.

Meid, Wolfgang. Obituary of Julius Pokorny. *Studia Celtica* 6 (1971): 196–97.

Morris-Jones, John. *A Welsh Grammar, Historical and Comparative.* Oxford: Clarendon, 1913.

————*Sir John Rhŷs.* The Sir John Rhŷs Memorial Inaugural Lecture. London: British Academy, 1925.

Parry, Thomas. *John Morris-Jones.* Cyfres Ddwyieithog Gŵyl Ddewi. Gwasg Prifysgol Cymru: Caerdydd, 1958.

Rhŷs, John. *Lectures on Welsh Philology.* Oxford, 1877.

Thurneysen, Rudolph. "Why Do Germans Study Celtic Philology?" *Studies* 14 (1930): 20–30.

Watkins, T. Arwyn. Obituary of Julius Pokorny. *Studia Celtica* 6 (1971): 195–96.

Williams, J. E. Caerwyn. "Syr John Morris-Jones—y cefndir a'r cyfnod cynnar." *Trafodion yr Anrhydeddus Gymdeithas y Cymmrodorion* 1965: 167–206; 1966: 16–72.

Williams, Waldo. "Yr Heriaith." In *The Oxford Book of Welsh Verse.* Ed. Thomas Parry. Oxford UP, 1962.

Death of a Schoolboy: The Early Greek Beginnings of a Crisis in Philology

GREGORY NAGY

In the earliest attested mention of schools in ancient Greece, Herodotus 6.27.2, the spotlight centers on an incident that occurred on the island of Chios around 496 B.C., where a roof collapsed on a group of 120 boys as they were being taught *grammata* "letters"; only one boy survived.[1] This disaster is explicitly described by Herodotus as an omen presaging the overall political disaster that was about to befall the whole community of Chios in the wake of the Ionian Revolt against the Persians (6.27.1), namely, the attack by Histiaios (6.26.1–2) and then the atrocities resulting from the occupation of the island by the Persians (6.31–32).

The disaster that befell the schoolboys at Chios is directly coupled by the narrative of Herodotus with another disaster, likewise presaging the overall political disaster about to befall all of Chios: at about the same time that the roof caved in on the boys studying their *grammata* 'letters' in school (again, 6.27.2), a *khoros* 'chorus' of 100 young men from Chios, officially sent to Delphi for a performance at a festival there, fell victim to a plague that killed 98 of them. Only two of the boys returned alive to Chios (*ibid.*).

In this account by Herodotus, then, we see two symmetrical disasters befalling the poetic traditions of a community, presaging a general political disaster befalling the community as a whole: first to be mentioned are the old-fashioned and élitist oral traditions of the chorus, to be followed by the newer and even more élitist written traditions of the school.[2] In what follows, I shall argue that the differentiation between the older and newer traditions, as we see it played out in the narrative of Herodotus, can be viewed as the beginnings of the crisis of philology, ongoing in our own time.

Let us begin with the older traditions. In pre-Classical Greece, the *khoros* 'chorus' was a specially selected group whose sacred task was to sing and dance at a given ritual occasion. The chorus represented, reenacted, the community of the polis or 'city state'. It was a formal communalization of the ritual experience by and for the community. The medium of the song and dance, commonly known as 'choral lyric,' was performed by non-professionals, for whom such performance was a ritual act of community.

The traditional restriction of choral lyric to performance by non-professionals indicates a less differentiated medium than, say, monodic lyric. From the standpoint of later Classical standards in the more differentiated world of poetic and musical professionalism, the inherited necessity of performance by a chorus of non-professionals imposed limitations on the virtuosity of both performance and composition (cf. "Aristotle," *Problems* 19.15). Moreover, the references to non-professional choral performance in Homeric and Hesiodic poetry, combined with cross-cultural comparative evidence, make it clear that the social institution of what we call the chorus even antedates the institution of the polis.[3]

The *khoros* was by nature a microcosm of society. The Spartans, for example, actually referred to the interior of their civic space as the *Khoros* (Pausanias 3.11.9). As a microcosm of society, the chorus was also a microcosm of social hierarchy. Within the chorus hierarchy, as the detailed investigation of Claude Calame has shown, a majority of younger members acted out a pattern of subordination to a minority of older leaders. The concept of older leaders, within the hierarchy of the chorus, was in most instances embodied in the central persona of the *khorêgos* 'chorus-leader'. There is a pervasive choral convention of emphasizing the superiority of the *khorêgos* and the subordination of the "I" that speaks for the choral aggregate; while the collectivity of the choral aggregate is itself egalitarian, the superiority of the *khorêgos* is a fundamental model of hierarchy.[4]

The acting-out of egalitarian and hierarchical relationships in the chorus amounted to an educational collectivization of experience.[5] In archaic Greece, it was the chorus that served as the social foundation of education, the Classical word for which is *paideiâ*. It is in this light that I propose to view the disaster of the plague that befell the chorus-boys from Chios. With the loss of a chorus of boys, a microcosm of the whole community of Chios is symbolically extinguished.

The Greek concept of *paid-* 'child' inherent in *paideiâ* 'education' includes girls as well as boys, and there is in fact a wealth of evidence from the archaic Greek period concerning the education of young girls through the medium of girls' choruses.[6] In this presentation, however, I shall be concentrating on boys' choruses, since it was this institution that became further differentiated: besides the older tradition of boys' choruses, there developed a relatively newer tradition of boys' schools. It is both these traditions, boys' choruses and boys' schools, that are reflected in the Herodotean account of the twin disasters that befell the community of Chios.

Before we proceed in chronological order from boys' chorus to boys' school, however, let us return for a moment to what we have observed so far about the chorus as a formal expression of both hierarchy and egalitarianism in the polis. We may add that the *khorêgos* 'chorus-leader' is diachronically a combination of composer and leading performer, while the rest of the *khoreutai* 'chorus-members' are performers. The key to choral performance is the public presentation, the *apodeixis*, of the *khorêgos* (cf. Herodotus 5.83.3). The authority of the *khorêgos* is literally *presented* through the performance of the "I" that is the chorus, and it is from this authority that his authorship emanates.

These considerations are pertinent to a pattern of evolution in the highly complex institution of the dramatic festivals, especially the Feast of the City Dionysia, in the polis of Athens. Here the *khorêgos* 'chorus-leader' has become ultimately differentiated as a contemporary non-performer, who organizes and subsidizes both the composition and the performance.[7] Meanwhile, the differentiated function of a *performing* chorus-leader is further differentiated by another split in functions, with a marked "first actor" on one hand and an unmarked chorus-leader on the other. This further differentiation is represented in the story that tells of Thespis' "invention" of the first actor.[8] A dialogue between the differentiated "first actor" and the undifferentiated chorus-leader would be a further differentiation of a dialogue between the *khorêgos* and the chorus.[9] Finally, there are yet further stages of differentiation with the "invention" of the "second actor," attributed to Aeschylus,[10] and of a "third actor," attributed to Sophocles.[11] The first actor, of course, is diachronically the

composer. Such was the situation with Aeschylus,[12] whereas with Sophocles there is further differentiation between composer and actor, in that
Sophocles, tradition has it, ceased to act in the later stages of his career.[13]

After having gone through this all-too-brief overview of complex patterns of differentiation, in Athenian drama, of the traditional interaction
of *khorêgos* 'chorus-leader' and *khoreutai* 'chorus-members', we may turn
back to the simplex point of departure, that is, the fundamental component of performance by the chorus. As is still evident in the idiom of
Attic Greek, the words *tragôidoi* 'performers of tragedy' and *kômôidoi* 'performers of comedy' refer not only to the choruses but also to the actual
performances of tragedy and comedy respectively.[14]

For the purposes of my presentation, I draw special attention to the
evolution from performer to non-performer in the case of Sophocles. The
case is particularly striking in view of what we know about earlier stages of
his career. At one point, Sophocles reportedly played the lyre himself
when he played the role of Thamyris in the *Thamyris,* and he played ball
with great skill when he played the role of Nausikaa in the *Nausikaa.*[15]
We may note also a report that Sophocles in his youth performed a dance,
naked and anointed with oil, to the accompaniment of his lyre, around
the trophy erected after the battle of Salamis;[16] whatever we may think
about the historicity of this account, its details point to a public choral
setting. I quote an apt summary: "In Sophocles the unity of poet, dancer,
and musician reaches its *akmê* among dramatists."[17]

With the differentiation of composer and performer, as illustrated by
the career of Sophocles, we see the beginnings of a disintegration that is
taking place in the very medium of the chorus, as formalized in choral
lyric. A clear sign of these beginnings is the institution of boys' schools,
where the performance of choral lyric could be taught apart from the boys'
chorus. If the chorus becomes dispensable in a school for performing
choral lyric, then the idea of the chorus as the primary medium of education will also have become dispensable. In which case, it is only a matter
of time before the performance itself of choral lyric becomes dispensable.
With the passage of time, the performance of choral lyric need no longer
be the primary curriculum of boys' schools. Thus the progression from an
old-fashioned education in the chorus towards an innovative education in
the school inexorably leads to still newer patterns of education in a school
that may no longer have anything to do with the chorus. The differentiated new concept of "schools" becomes further differentiated into "old

schools," which had taught the performance of choral lyric, and "new schools," with a curriculum emancipated from the medium of chorus altogether.

By the time of the late fifth century, in a rapidly changing polis like Athens, schools were in fact becoming divorced from the traditions of performance in choral lyric. A prime example is the school of Socrates as ridiculed in the *Clouds* of Aristophanes. Explicitly contrasted in the *Clouds* is the old-fashioned Athenian *paideiâ* 'education', the kind that purportedly produced the men who fought at the Battle of Marathon (τὴν ἀρχαίαν παιδείαν, l. 961).[18] Back in those glory days, schoolboys learned selected compositions of old lyric masters in the house of the *kitharistês* 'master of the *kitharâ*' (964), who taught them to learn by heart (966) the performance of famous lyric compositions (967) and who insisted on their adherence to performing these compositions in the proper *harmoniâ* 'accordatura' that had been "inherited from their ancestors" (968; cf. 969–72).

The *Clouds* of Aristophanes draws a sharp contrast between this old *paideiâ* 'education' and the "modern" schooling that the figure of Pheidippides has just received from Socrates and his disciples. In *Clouds* 1353–58, we find the figure of Strepsiades berating his son Pheidippides for using his new education to ridicule the traditions of old-fashioned liberal education in the "Classics." On the occasion of a symposium, Pheidippides had refused a request to take up the lyre and sing a famous lyric composition by Simonides (*Clouds* 1355–56). The composition was a choral lyric, a victory ode (Simonides PMG 507). To engage in the monodic performance of choral masterpieces was an old-fashioned convention at symposia, as we can see from such references as the present passage from the *Clouds*.

It is clear that Phedippides is not well-versed in the art form of this kind of performance. Perhaps the most celebrated example of this theme is in Cicero *Tusculan Disputations* 1.4, on the embarrassment of the great statesman Themistokles in being unable, at a symposium, to sing and accompany himself on the lyre. As for Pheidippides, after he refuses to perform the choral lyric of Simonides, he is asked at least to perform something from the compositions of Aeschylus, while holding a branch of myrtle (*Clouds* 1365). Of course it is not the lyre but the *aulos* 'reed' that serves as the medium of accompaniment for the choral lyric compositions of Athenian Drama. Singing to the lyre implies potential self-accompaniment, whereas singing to the *aulos* does not. Thus there is a lower degree of education required for performing in the chorus of an Aeschylean tragedy or for re-performing at a symposium selections from the choral songs of such a tragedy. Even this kind of performance is refused by Pheidippides, who elects to recite a passage from a speech in Euripides (*Clouds* 1371). The word *rhêsis* 'speech' (*ibid.*) makes it clear that the modern Pheidippides opts for a medium that is devoid of the lyric element.

The nostalgic glimpse of old-fashioned *paideiâ* 'education' in the *Clouds* of Aristophanes, looking back to the days of Marathon, the same era reflected in the Herodotean account of the learning of *grammata* 'letters' by schoolboys in Chios, provides us with a basis for understanding the gradual metamorphosis of schooling in the performance of the "Classics." The oral traditions of the chorus are giving way to the written traditions of the school.

And yet, the evolution of ancient Greek canons in both poetry and song need not be attributed primarily to the factor of writing. I grant that writing would have been essential for the ultimate preservation of these canons once the traditions of performance were becoming obsolete, but the key to the actual evolution of canons must be sought in the social context of performance itself. The performance-traditions of the Classics, as an extension of the canonization of oral traditions in poetry and song, were preserved in the social context of private education for the élite.

For the Greek city-states, the ancestral mode of education was public, through the performance of song and poetry at festivals. In the case of poetry, performance at festivals tended to be left to professionals such as the rhapsodes at the festival of the Panathenaia at Athens. In the case of song, the situation was more complex, as in the case of a festival like the City Dionysia at Athens, where poetry was performed by professional actors while song was performed by the non-professional chorus. Here the performance by the chorus was a central form of civic education, not only for the audience at large but also for the members of the chorus themselves. The numbers of chorus-members selected each year for the annual production of the City Dionysia convey the pervasiveness of the institution: for example, the three competing choruses of the tragedies required a total of not less than thirty-six new chorus members each year, while the ten competing choruses of the dithyrambs, with separate men's and boys' divisions, added up to a yearly total of 500 men and 500 boys.[19] Wherever the traditions of making song and poetry are still alive, as in the docu-

mented cases of the City Dionysia and the Panathenaia, we have reason
to think that the process of civic education through song and poetry is
also alive.

And yet, the traditions of songmaking and poetry at the City Dionysia
tended to absorb or displace older traditions of songmaking and poetry,
such as those represented by Simonides. And here we see a fundamental
impetus for the very institution of private schools: if public education in
the older traditions of songmaking was becoming less and less available
by way of the chorus, since the State was transforming the old aristocratic poetics into the new popular poetics of the City Dionysia, then
the older ways of choral education in the older traditions of songmaking
had to be compensated by way of private schooling for the élite. Once
State Theater, the creation of tyrants, becomes transformed into the
democratic self-expression of the polis, the concept of the private school
can become the non-democratic self-expression of aristocrats, the new
breeding-ground of tyrants.[20]

Even private schools, however, serve as a setting for changes in the old
traditions of songmaking. In the older poetics, we would naturally expect
the traditions of composition-in-performance to survive from one generation to the next through the factor of performance. And yet, if the
traditions of composition-in-performance were breaking down, then the
need for sample performances would become greater and greater. Which
means that education itself would become gradually transformed: the
learning of techniques in composition through performance could shift to
the learning of sample compositions through reading. Once the performance tradition becomes obsolete, the text is no longer a demonstration
of ability to perform: rather, the text becomes simply a sample piece of
writing, potentially there to be imitated by other sample pieces of writing.

Still, the written text can present itself as not just a sample composition
but a sample composition *as potential performance*. It is a privately teach-
able demonstration of what could be publicly performed, and its accessibil-
ity depends on power, political power. To gain access to such a sample
composition is to gain knowledge, from a privileged vantage point. The
composition, as a mimesis of re-composition in public performance, is a
paradigm of authority that is as hard to come by as some treasure in a
treasure-box, accessible to the rich and powerful. The silent reading of
such a sample composition, such a "script," is symptomatic of the tyrant's
power to control the performance of a composition. The reading out loud

of such a script, by contrast, is the metaphor for performance, and in fact the very act of reading out loud is the ultimate metaphor of State Theater.

With the increasing complexity of society in the context of the polis comes a pattern of differentiation in the passing on of traditions from generation to generation, and the institution of schools, as we have seen it described in the Aristophanic passage about the good old days of *paideiâ* 'education' in the era of the Battle of Marathon, may be considered a reflex of this pattern. Already in this era, schools are not a phenomenon merely confined to Athens but seem to appear throughout archaic Greece, as we see from our point of departure, the report in Herodotus 6.27.2 relating the incident that occurred in Chios around 496 B.C., when the roof collapsed on the 120 boys as they were being taught *grammata* 'letters'.

That the *grammata* 'letters' being taught to these select boys of Chios correspond to our notion of "belles-lettres" or liberal education in song and poetry is made clear if we compare the portrait of education in the *Protagoras* of Plato. Here again, however, as in the *Clouds* of Aristophanes, this kind of education is in fact considered no longer new but already old-fashioned.

In the *Protagoras*, with its dramatization of the way things supposedly had been in the second half of the fifth century, we can see how schooling is a matter of differentiations in the passing on of traditions from generation to generation. The subject is introduced as we find an old Protagoras debating with Socrates in a company of young Athenian intellectuals that pointedly includes two sons of Pericles himself (314e). In his description of *paideiâ*, the figure of Protagoras specifically says that the wealthy can afford more of it: they extend the education of their boys by starting it earlier and continuing it longer (326c).[21] There are at least three stages to what Protagoras describes. First, there is a period of education at home, where father, mother, *trophos* 'nurse', and *paidagôgos* 'tutor' all play a role in one's early ethical *formation* (325cd). Second, the boy is sent to school, where he is taught letters for the explicit purpose of memorizing poetry (325e–326a); that this memorization is for the explicit purpose of performing and interpreting this poetry is made clear in Protagoras' description of the third stage of schooling, where the child is taught to sing compositions of lyric poets while accompanying himself to the lyre (326ab). Whereas the poetry that is taught in the earlier stage is described only generally as *diexodoi, epainoi,* and *enkômia* concerning 'noble men of the past' (326a), the poetry taught at the later stage is specifically lyric poetry (the compositions of *melopoioi* 'lyric poets': *ibid.*). From the standpoint of Protagoras, the most important aspect of *paideiâ* (his word) is to acquire skill in the performance and interpretation of poetry (339a), and it is clear that he is thinking in particular of song, that is, lyric poetry: illustrating his point about the primacy of poetry in education, he begins his debate with Socrates by citing and then interpreting a lyric composition of Simonides (339b and following: Simonides PMG 542), having just made an earlier reference to a famous lyric passage from Pindar (337d: Pindar F 169a.1–5 SM).

After Protagoras and Socrates have a contest of wits in interpreting the meaning of the composition by Simonides (and Socrates comes off with the seemingly superior interpretation), Alcibiades challenges Protagoras to continue his debate with Socrates by abandoning the use of poetry as the framework for the discussion (347b and 348b), in the context of a particularly significant remark of Socrates: to use poetry as a framework for the debate between Protagoras and himself is analogous, says Socrates, to the hiring of girl-musicians, either string or wind, or girl-dancers to entertain at symposia (347cd). Such participants in the symposium reveal their lack of *paideiâ* 'education' (ἀπαιδευσία: 347c), whereas those who are noble and 'educated' (πεπαιδευμένοι) can entertain themselves with their own conversations (347d). Plato could have had Socrates say, as does the poetry of Aristophanes, that the educated participants in the symposium can also entertain themselves by performing and interpreting lyric compositions, as opposed to the ill-educated participants who hire girl-musicians to play for them. But of course Plato is the champion of a new education where dialogue supplants the primacy of poetry, and Socrates in fact goes on to set up "the poets" as a bad thing that is parallel to the girl-musicians (347e). In other words, instead of having girl-musicians as a foil for "the poets," Plato has both the girl-musicians and "the poets" serving together as a foil for the medium of the dialogue that Socrates and Alcibiades are advocating.

The stance of Alcibiades here is particularly suggestive: his is the generation ridiculed in the *Clouds* of Aristophanes for abandoning the ideals of old-fashioned *paideiâ*. According to these ideals, as we have seen, a sign of the highest achievement was the performance, at a symposium, of a lyric composition by one of the old masters. There is a vivid contrast to these ideals in the *Alcibiades* of Plutarch (2.6), where the young Alcibiades refuses to learn how to play the reed: let the Thebans, says he, play the reed, since *they* do not know how to have a conversation at a symposium.

In the end, we are left with what? We see the girl-musicians being excluded from the company of good old boys. Even as slave-girls, women lose the chance to contribute to, let alone benefit from, the new *paideiâ*. Meanwhile, the traditions of the old *paideiâ*, where aristocratic girls had once received their education in the form of choral training, becomes obsolete. Obsolete too, ironically, is the old *paideiâ* of boys, both in the chorus and in the schools. The new schools seem to have lost the art of performing the "Classics," and the Classics have become written texts to be studied and emulated in writing. Gone forever are the performances of Sophocles. Gone forever is the possibility of bringing such performances back to life, even if for just one more time, at occasions like the symposium. Gone forever, perhaps, is the art of actually performing a composition for any given occasion.

It may be that the very concept of *genre* becomes necessary only when the *occasion* for a given speech-act, that is, for the performance of a given poem or song, is lost. Such is the case with the scholar-poets of the Hellenistic era: "so they composed hymns to the gods, without any idea of performing them, or they wrote epitaphs, without any idea of inscribing them on a gravestone, or they wrote symposiastic poetry, without any real drinking-party in mind."[22]

It is this brave new world of the Hellenistic period, the era of the great Library of Alexandria, that gives us the word *philologos*, 'philologist'. The first to use this title was reportedly Eratosthenes of Cyrene, who succeeded the scholar-poet Apollonius of Rhodes as head of the Library.[23] Yet this same era reflects a nostalgia for the Muses of performance: the very name of the Library was the Museum, the place of the Muses, and its head was officially a priest of the Muses, nominated by the king himself.[24] The members of the Museum, which was part of the royal palace, have been described as follows:

> They had a carefree life: free meals, high salaries, no taxes to pay, very pleasant surroundings, good lodgings and servants. There was plenty of opportunity for quarrelling with each other.[25]

One might say that the Museum itself was a formalization of nostalgia for the glory days when the Muses supposedly inspired the poet's performance.

Another head of the Alexandrian library, Aristarchus of Samothrace, perhaps the most accomplished philologist of the Hellenistic era, was described by Panaetius of Rhodes, a leading figure among the Stoics, as a *mantis* 'seer' when it came to understanding poetry (Athenaeus xiv 634c). In this concept of the seer we see again the nostalgia of philology for the Muses of inspired performance.

The beginnings of the split that had led to this nostalgia, ongoing into our own time, are evident from our point of departure, the doubling of the omens presaging the misfortune that befell the community of Chios. It is as if the misfortune of the Chiotes had to be presaged separately, in both public and private sectors. The deaths of the chorus-boys affected the public at large, in that choruses were inclusive, to the extent that they represented the community at large. The deaths of the schoolboys, on the other hand, affected primarily the élite, in that schools were exclusive, restricted to the rich and the powerful.

For our own era, the scene of a disaster where the roof caves in on schoolboys learning their letters becomes all the more disturbing because schools are all we have left from the split between the more inclusive education of the chorus and the more exclusive education of the school. For us it is not just a scene: it is a primal scene. The crisis of philology, signaled initially by the split between chorus and school, deepens with the narrowing of *paideiâ* over the course of time. The symptom of a narrowed education is the terminal prestige of arrested development, where schoolboys grow up to be the old boys of a confraternity that they call philology, *their* philology.[26] The hope lies in the capacity of true philology, as also of schools, to reverse such narrowing, to recover a more integrated, integral, *paideiâ*. The humanism of philology depends, and will always depend, on its inclusiveness.[27]

Harvard University

NOTES

1. We may compare the anecdote recorded by Pausanias 6.9.6 about the mass murder of 60 boys in a school at Astypalaea in 492 B.C.; the perpetrator was a frustrated athlete who had just come home to Astypalaea after having been disqualified at a boxing match at the Olympics: in a fit of rage, he reportedly brought down a pillar supporting the roof of the

school where the boys were learning. For another anecdote about a mass slaughter of schoolboys, see Thucydides 7.29.5.

2. The symbolism of these symmetrical disasters is signaled by the words *prosêmainein* 'make a sign [*sêma*] in advance' at Herodotus 6.27.1 (cf. also *sêmêia megala* 'mighty signs' *ibid.*). On the use of the word *sêma* 'sign, hero's tomb' in Herodotus for the purpose of signaling a symbol in the narrative, see G. Nagy, "The Sign of Protesilaos," *MHTIC: Revue d'anthropologie du monde grec ancien. Philologie. Histoire. Archéologie* 2 (1987): 207–13.

3. A fundamental work in this regard is C. Calame, *Les choeurs de jeunes filles en Grèce archaïque* I: *Morphologie, fonction religieuse et sociale.* II: *Alcman* (Rome 1977).

4. Cf. Calame I: 437–39.

5. Cf. Calame I: 437–39.

6. Calame's book, in fact, concentrates on girls' choruses as distinct from boys' and men's choruses.

7. For a review of the facts, see Calame I: 92–93.

8. Aristotle in Themistius *Orations* 26.316d; Charon of Lampsacus FGH 262 F 15; cf. A. Pickard-Cambridge, *The Dramatic Festivals of Athens,* 2nd ed. revised by J. Gould and D. M. Lewis (Oxford: Clarendon P, 1968) 130–31.

9. Cf. Aristotle, *Poetics,* 1456a25.

10. Aristotle, *Poetics,* 1449a15.

11. Aristotle, *Poetics,* 1449a15. For another version, see Pickard-Cambridge 131.

12. Cf., e.g., Athenaeus 21e–22a and the comments of Pickard-Cambridge 250–51.

13. Testimonia in Pickard-Cambridge 130 and n. 4.

14. Pickard-Cambridge 127–32.

15. Athenaeus 20e–f; commentary in Pickard-Cambridge 251.

16. Athenaeus 20e–f.

17. W. Mullen, *Choreia: Pindar and Dance* (Princeton, NJ: Princeton UP, 1982) 20.

18. The "old" παίδευσις 'education' (*Clouds* 986) is associated with the era that produced the fighters at Marathon (985–86).

19. Pickard-Cambridge 234–36.

20. In Herodotus, we find traces of a general attitude that the medium of writing encourages the private possession of the public media of singing and making speeches: for Herodotus, such private possession is a characteristic of tyrants: cf. F. Hartog, *Le miroir d'Hérodote: Essai sur la représentation de l'autre* (Paris, 1980) 287–88.

21. On this kind of élitism within the social context of the polis, see, e.g., Demosthenes, *On the Crown* 265.

22. G. Williams, *Tradition and Originality in Roman Poetry* (Oxford: Clarendon P, 1968) 35.

23. Suetonius, *De grammaticis et rhetoribus* 10.

24. Testimonia collected by R. Pfeiffer, *History of Classical Scholarship: From the Beginnings to the End of the Hellenistic Age* (Oxford: Clarendon P, 1968) 96.

25. Pfeiffer 97.

26. On the concept *terminal prestige,* see S. McClary, "Terminal Prestige: The Case of Avant-Garde Music Composition," *Cultural Critique* 12 (1989) 57–81.

27. Parts of this essay appear in a longer version: G. Nagy, "Ancient Greek Views of Poets and Poetry," in G. Kennedy, ed., *Cambridge History of Literary Criticism* I (Cambridge, Cambridge UP, 1989) 1–77. There is an even larger and more elaborated version in G. Nagy, *Pindar's Homer: The Lyric Possession of an Epic Past* (Baltimore: Johns Hopkins UP, 1990).

Anti-Foundational Philology

JONATHAN CULLER

For me, and I dare say for many others who are not philologists, the way in which I most frequently encounter philology is in the library as that ubiquitous P that appears on so many of the books I am searching for. In the Library of Congress catalogue system philology appears as the P that begins with "Language in general," P, and runs from PA, "Classical languages and literatures," through such exotic subdivisions as PM ("Hyperborean and American Indian languages and literature and Artificial languages"—a curious combination), all the way to PZ, "Fiction in English," the very bottom of the philological heap. Our question is what is at stake in philology and the simple answer is the empire of the *P's*. As Gregory Nagy says in the previous essay, it is a question of power: who shall reign in the kingdom of the *P's*, how shall it be divided?

Philology has a relational identity; it depends on what it is opposed to, so the question what is philology is the question of what are the relevant oppositions that divide, delimit, articulate the domain of the *P's*. Which are the books that belong to the philologists and which to the non-philologists? Naturally, those who consider themselves philologists wish to have some of the better books on their side, and those who have used philology as a whipping boy have sought to relegate to its domain what they take to be duller and less productive works of linguistic and literary scholarship. Definitions range from the broadest, the comprehensive study of cultures, to the narrowest, the study of the language of certain texts from the past. Barbara Johnson and several other contributors to this issue have referred to Walter Jackson Bate's article on "The Crisis in English Studies," which sets up an opposition with philology, understood as historical language study, on the one side, and on the other side literary study attuned to or focused on such compelling human issues as the moral greatness of Samuel Johnson and John Keats. Characteristically, the proponents of any approach will be disinclined to accept the oppositions used by others to characterize them. In his essay, Professor Simon speaks of the conception of philology as historical language study as a perversion, a caricature. However, it seems to me that it is a description that responds rather well to a conception of philology put forward by the philologists themselves. This is the notion of philology as basic or foundational, a kind of first knowledge that serves as the precondition of any further literary criticism or historical and interpretive work. It seems to me that it is this notion of philology as basic that needs to be questioned here. That questioning could take the form of identifying various ways in which philological activity and especially the reconstruction of cultures performed by philology turns out to be itself based on concepts or schemes that philology as the art of reading slowly ought to help us put in question. The critique of the notion of the foundational character of philology would take the form, in other words, of showing how philological projects rely uncritically on literary and cultural conceptions that come from the domains of thought that are supposedly secondary.

Let me briefly sketch a number of versions of this argument. First, several contributors emphasize the basic philological project of reconstructing the meaning of a word, particularly in ancient texts. This activity depends on a crucial enabling convention, which itself has the character not of a fact of nature but of a cultural assumption, one of many possible cultural conventions about the nature of texts, namely the assumption that the word has a meaning, and that this meaning is something one can reconstruct by the means that philology has available to it. Frequently, of course, the activity of reconstruction relies on further assumptions about the relation between the meaning of a word and the further constructions which we call the beliefs of a culture. If one tries to imagine reconstructing the meaning of a word in a poem by John Ashbery on the basis of a hypothesis about what twentieth-century Americans believe, one gains some idea about difficulty of thinking of the philological enterprise as in some sense foundational, prior to other interpretive

work. On the contrary, such philological investigation is profoundly dependent on conceptions of a culture and theories about the nature of
literary practices and literary conventions.

A second example might come from what has been a particularly
impotant philological activity, the reconstruction of texts, the proposing
of emendations, when texts seem as though they might be corrupt. Frequently, of course, emendations from the past, even when proposed by
the most famous philologists of their day, seem to us to tell us more about
the culture and assumptions of the philologists, the deficiencies in their
understanding or ability to appreciate the otherness of a text, than they
do about the original text itself. Bentley is a case in point: a learned
philologist, whose work on Milton now seems not foundational scholarship but interpretation determined by a certain framework of assumptions
from his own culture. Here too, then, philological activity seems to be
based on certain kinds of literary and interpretive notions rather than
serving as their basis.

A third case might be the example John Koch cites in his essay on the
Celtic philologists. His very interesting discussion stresses the fact that
the objectives of the philologist and the language movement were one
and the same. The project of reconstructing Celtic tradition was very
much governed by notions of what Celtic cultures ought to be, an attempt, as he puts it, not to reconstruct a monument from the past but to
restore a functioning system. The philological enterprise here is governed
by the idea of producing a living culture.

A fourth example might be the question of how far the construction of
philology as a scientific discipline in the late eighteenth and early nineteenth century was complicitous with or was based on the invention of an
Aryan Greece that would serve as origin for modern cultures in northern
Europe. The invention of that Greece involves the rejection or elimina-
tion of the idea of Greece's dependence on Semitic cultures and on Egypt
in particular. This is another case in which one could argue that the
supposedly foundational enterprise of philology is in fact dependent on
cultural and aesthetic constructions. Clearly it seemed much more satisfy-
ing to European cultures to have Greek rather than Egyptian origins.

Finally one might cite the case Gregory Nagy mentions in his essay of
important philological work on Homeric poetry, which is based to a
considerable extent on Albert Lord's work on modern Yugoslavian oral
epics. The interpretation of a contemporary literary practice is what pro-

vides the model for an extremely important ancient philological project of
reconstruction.

My point, then, would be simply that the notion of philology as a basis
which is somehow prior to literary and cultural interpretation is an idea
that one should seriously question, and an idea, moreover, that philology
itself, in principle as well as in practice, provides us with the tools for
questioning. For if there is one thing that runs through the various accounts of philology and the various accounts in which philology figures it
is the linking of philology with close attention to language. That attention is particularly valuable, as Barbara Johnson stresses, in its potential to
display language as something more than meaning, as structures which
can be described prior to the meaning they produce, prior to the meaning
that is conferred on them. There is in philology, then, a tension between
the reconstructive project—especially important in cases of minority
cultures—and the valuable attention to what undermines the aesthetic
and ideological assumptions about the meaning of texts on which reconstructive projects depend. The assumption that Latin apostrophes are
sacral in character is just an example of one of these reconstructive assumptions on which philology has relied but that it is the task of philology
to dismantle and expose. The play of the term *philology*, it seems to me, is
valuable insofar as it captures the crucial tension between the reconstructive project and that critique of construction which philology ought to
have as its goal.

Cornell University

Greek Philology: Diversity and Difference

MARGARET ALEXIOU

"Our attitude to the past is always determined by the position we take up in facing our present and our future. And *vice versa,* our attitude to the present and future is fully expressed by our conception of the past. There is no exception to this—not even the sound scholar with his supposed detachment and objectivity."[1]

If Bachtin's premise is correct—namely, that philology is not an eternal, unchanging entity, but that both its theory and praxis have been constantly refashioned in accordance with changing perceptions of the past—then there is every reason to be optimistic about its future, provided that its role in the present debate in the Humanities can be frankly addressed, and provided that past assumptions can be viewed in their historical context. As Bachtin's work has shown, Greek philology offers an exceptionally rich—if contentious—field for such an analysis. First and foremost, the Greek language (and with it, its metaphorical and cultural building-blocks) has retained its dynamic cohesion as an isolated member of the Indo-European family of languages for over three millennia, despite historical upheavals and cultural interactions with neighbouring Balkan and Anatolian peoples throughout the history and prehistory of Greece. A second, and equally cogent, argument for the relevance of Greece to the current debate concerns the marginalisation of its post-classical cultures, which places it—paradoxically—at the very center of critical discourse. Situated at the intersection of East and West, with a classical heritage appropriated by the West as an idealised image of its own civilised origins, but also with medieval and modern cultures which do not always conform to Western patterns of development, Greece can become a test case for the validity of scholarly assumptions on both sides of the critical fence. Third, since Greece is a young and developing nation-state, Greek scholars and speakers alike will have a significant voice in shaping the future of Greek philology. In other words, the matter is not one for purely academic debate.

Perhaps the most crucial issue in the so-called crisis in the Humanities concerns not philology itself, but the politics of the literary canon, and—of course—the politics of its deconstruction. Inevitably, with the internationalisation of literary curricula and the rise of comparative studies, and with the growing number of "minority" practitioners (including women), the traditionally dominant position of Western "masterworks" has not gone unchallenged: women's literature, Afro-American literature, Hispanic and South American literature (to name but a few) are gaining recognition across American campuses. It is a development which should be welcomed as an encouragement to broaden and sharpen our perceptions of language and literature, rather than resisted as a threat to the "fabric of Western civilisation," since studies of strong oral cultures of today—which have already shed invaluable light on the nature and functions of poetry in pre-modern societies—can now be undertaken on a more scholarly and truly comparative basis. At the same time, the very concepts of philology and literary criticism as self-justifying, objective, and humanising pursuits have been challenged by post-structuralist theorists of many colors who have sought to uncover the political and institutional mechanisms of inclusion and exclusion which have traditionally determined both the literary canon and the modes of its analysis.

We philologists are therefore faced with a series of choices. At one extreme, we may try to opt out of the debate and take refuge in entrenched positions: philology entails above all the correct establishment and comprehension of the text; therefore it is the *sine qua non* of all literary interpretation, a precise, dispassionate, and scientific discipline, to be compared with anatomy in the medical sciences; moreover, it provides an excellent training for the mind which can act as an antidote to noxious ideologies and -isms. At the other extreme, we may be tempted to jump on the bandwagon of certain post-structuralist schools and to dismiss old forms of textual criticism, philological analysis, and literary commentary as outmoded and elitist examples of self-indulgent empiricism, in order to engage ourselves instead with theoretical issues of literature as discourse and the inevitable violence of all forms of representation. The politics of philology—as, indeed, of all academic disciplines—is a reality, it is around, whether we recognise it or not.

The trouble with the former argument, that the philologist's words—like the anatomist's bodies or the archaeologists' bones and stones—are a matter for scientific analysis, not to be disputed, is that words tend to change over time, even to decompose and recompose. Unless texts are to be treated as cadavers or lifeless artifacts, selection and interpretation are required in the process of their reconstitution, and this is where the germs of literary theory may set in. It is also where diachronic studies of the Greek language become directly relevant to Greek philology. The differences between modern Greek and classical Greek have been calculated as roughly comparable with those between modern English and Chaucerian English; those between modern Greek and Homeric Greek no greater than those between modern English and the language of Beowulf; meantime the Hellenistic *koine* (the language of the Septuagint, the New Testament, and many papyrus letters and non-literary inscriptions) is closer to modern Greek than it is to Homeric Greek.[2] It follows that modern Greek should be as indispensable an aid to the classicist as modern English is natural for Chaucerian and Anglo-Saxon scholars of all ethnicities, with the additional argument that, in the case of Greek, almost all ancient literature has been selected, transcribed, and transmitted, with scholia, by Alexandrian and Byzantine scholars, for whom the interference of post-classical forms of Greek can be shown to have played a major part in errors of transcription and interpretation.[3] To resume the medical metaphor, to cut off the ancient literature from its medieval transmitters and its living present is the philological equivalent of the anatomical practice of lobectomy or the medical condition of skotoma. The germs of living organisms may be preferable after all.

The trouble with the post-structuralists' case begins with the impenetrability of their verbal pyrotechnics for all but the initiated few, and is symptomatic of their determination to "professionalise" the study of language and literature. In practice, this has often led to a divorce between life and literature, a denigration of the role of human emotions in artistic composition and reception, and a reduction of scholarship to an academic power game. Many of their theoretical underpinnings are rooted in Western concepts of anxiety, guilt, and violence which have little relevance for non-Western and pre-modern cultures. Least attractive is their frequent tone of self-congratulatory superiority, or aggressive complacency, whereby different approaches may be summarily dismissed as traditional, empiricist, or historicist.

Fortunately, there are many people—including creative writers—who reject the current polarisation between Philology and Theory as false, and seek, not a middle way, but a different kind of solution. Some comments on the history of the word *philologia* itself can provide an excellent starting point. In ancient Greek, its range of meanings include "love of argument, reasoning" (Plato); "learned conversation" (Antigonos Karystios, *apud* Athenaios); "love of learning, literature" (Isokrates, Aristotle: see Liddell-Scott-Jones *s. v.*). It re-entered the Greek vocabulary during the later seventeenth century as the equivalent of Latin *litteratura,* inclusive of all kinds of writing (history, theology, philosopohy, even the natural sciences) until in the eighteenth century it was narrowed down to "imaginative, creative writing," a sense it retained until 1886, when a new term, *logotechnia* ("word-craft") was coined by the demoticists on the model of the German *Nazional-Literatur* (1779) in their attempt to wrest literary hegemony from the purists.[4] Today, *philologia* is used primarily in the sense of the "study of literature" (as opposed to *logotechnia,* the "practice of literature"), and as such is retained in universities for all literary courses, Greek and foreign. In popular speech, however—especially in the plural—it has the pejorative sense of "clever but useless and irrelevant talk." In English, *philology* is first recorded in 1614 in the ancient sense of "love of learning and literature," acquiring the meaning of "science of language" only in 1716, a usage now subsumed under *linguistics* (1837). But it was above all in Germany towards the end of the eighteenth century that *Philologie* became associated with *Alterthumswissenschaft,* or the "scientific" study of the ancient (Greek) world. The history of the word—especially outside Greece—therefore reveals a steady erosion of its wider ancient meanings to "writings," "creative writings," "science of language"—so where do we go from here?

It is time to revive the older senses of *philologia* before it disappears altogether, or is reduced to its modern colloquial sense. The increasing specialisation of disciplines within the Humanities since the end of the Enlightenment has brought with it the assumption that, as a result, the study of language and literature has become more scientific. How true is this, and what changes may we expect to see over the next decades? To date, philology has been a Western and male-dominated preserve, particularly in the Classics. While the study of etymologies, semantic changes, morphological and syntactic structures, and the interrelatedness of different languages and language groups can never become obsolete, a broadening of perspectives must surely follow the steady increase in the numbers of women and minority practioners in Western universities, and the incipient increase in the quality and quantity of scholars from outside the hallowed Western seats of learning, who are beginning to question the origins of our civilisation from the comparativist perspective of their own—often equally ancient and civilised—past. There will be a new awareness of the relevance of issues such as gender, nationism, and race.

First, gender. Examples of sexist fantasy and bias in philological studies abound; but the prize should probably go to the Welsh philologist Rowland Jones. In his tract *The Origins of Languages and Nations* (1764/1972), written under the spell of Rousseau, Jones argues that the biblical name *Adam* comes, not from the Hebrew, but from the Celtic *had-am, ad-am,* meaning "seed of man"; while *Eve* means "him" because she was taken out of him. Similarly, Latin *mulier* is traced to Celtic *ma-il-wr* ("great race of man"), and *woman* means "animal from man." *Wife* is said to be a possessive form *w-y-fi,* or "my animal." Even the letters of the alphabet are given a sexual symbolism: *e* depicts the clitoris, *v* the vagina, *g* the testicles, *f* the penis in action, *p* flaccidity, *o* human sexuality at its most active, and so on.[5] Of course it is easy to make fun of such nonsense, but Jones is by no means untypical of his age during the early years of philology as "the science of language." Rather than react to such violations by littering our vocabulary with neologisms such as "chairperson" or "penpersonship," feminists today need only go back to the ancient languages to discover that Indo-European terminations were not originally marked for gender, but rather for differing—and complementary—categories of animate and inanimate forces.[6]

Second, nationist bias has also been apparent, in Greek no less than in Welsh. One example must suffice: the phrase *ares mares koukounares* (meaning "arrant nonsense") was derived by the Greek philologist A. Papadopoulos from ancient Greek *ara* ("curse"), *mara* (*maraino,* "wither") and—correctly—modern *koukounara* ("pine-nut" AG *kokkon*), without reference to the common Turkish expressive reduplicative pattern *kitap-*

mitap ("books and the like"), *kafe-mafe* ("coffee and such"). Nationist rules for interpreting etymologies are formulated by K. Amantos, another philologist of the early twentieth century: "It is not permissible method-ologically to seek foreign loan words when we can derive etymologies from the Greek."[7] Slavic and above all Turkish influence is to be denied or minimised at all costs.

It is safe to deride the sexist bias of an eighteenth-century Welshman and the nationalist bias of a twentieth-century Greek. But what about our own preconceptions? They have been fundamentally challenged by Martin Bernal's recent book, *Black Athena: The Afro-Asiatic Roots of Classical Civilisation*, volume 1, *The Fabrication of Ancient Greece 1785–1985* (1987). Despite the fact that his work has been dismissed informally in classical circles as "mad, bad and dangerous to know" (as Lady Caroline Lamb once said of Lord Byron), there has as yet been no serious refutation from a philological perspective of his major thesis, which is as important— and perhaps more far-reaching—than Edward Said's *Orientalism* (1978). Scholars may disagree with this or that detail in his projected outline of the next two volumes, which will be concerned with archaeological and linguis-tic evidence for Egyptian and Phoenician elements in ancient Greek lan-guage and civilisation. However, his historiographical documentation has not been refuted: what he calls the "ancient model" (how the ancients viewed their own indebtedness to near Eastern neighbours) was rejected by philologists in favour of the "Aryan model" (the ancient Greeks were racially and linguistically pure Indo-Europeans, as a result of Dorian con-quests from the North) from the turn of the eighteenth and nineteenth centuries, and for ideological reasons motivated by Romantic Hellenism, racism, and imperialism. Ancient Greece has been appropriated to a West-ern image of its own civilised origins. The marginalisation—or exclusion— of modern Greece from this vision of Hellenism coincides perfectly with the process, and finds its most extreme expression in the attacks on the racial purity of the modern Greeks by the Austrian historian Jakob von Fallmerayer (1830 and 1836), who claimed that as a result of Slavic and Albanian incursions into Greece during the early middle ages, not a drop of pure Hellenic blood now flows in Greek veins. If we apply Bernal's thesis to the modern Greek question, we can replace the "Aryan model" of ancient Greece as linguistically and racially pure and unified with the "revised ancient model" as one of racial, linguistic, and cultural intermingling of near Eastern peoples in the prehistoric period, and extend the model diachronically to Byzantine, Ottoman, and modern Greece, where the focus of cultural interaction in the Greek-speaking world has shifted, expanded, and contracted, but where Balkan, Mediterranean, and Anatolian cultures have remained relevant throughout most of Greek history.

The case against traditional Indo-European philology is argued independently, and from a different perspective, by Colin Renfrew, in his *Archaeology and Language* (Cambridge UP, 1987). While his own thesis for the diffusion of Indo-European languages as a result of the spread of agriculture (cultivation of wheat) may be open to debate, Indo-European philologists cannot afford to ignore his challenge to some of their conclusions and underlying assumptions. He points out that the major theories for the origins and diffusion of Indo-European languages are based on outmoded, linear concepts of divergence (the "tree model"), and that archaeology, linguistics, and mythology has each tended to draw its conclusions from the hypotheses of the other by a process of mutually reinforcing circular argumentation. While accepting the traditional definition of Indo-European languages, he suggests that the "tree model" should be revised and modified in conjunction with the "wave model," and in accordance with the "processual" approach of more recent archaeology. Thus, areas of contiguity among non-related peoples are seen as potentially significant, especially when and where supported by archaeological and other evidence for cultural borrowings, while the "processual" approach is to be preferred to the structuralist one because it gives priority to known socio-economic changes among indigenous peoples. Pottery types and burial systems cannot be equated with language and ethnicity, nor need linguistic and ethnic change be explained in terms of foreign penetration or large-scale migration. Neither philology nor mythology is immune from the processes of history; meanwhile, attempts to explain the supposed difference between peace-loving peoples with a matristic pantheon and warlike peoples with a male-dominated and sky-oriented pantheon of warrior gods in terms of deep penetration of horse-riding Kurgans amount, like many other such theories, to no more than sheer fantasy.[8]

The question of continuity needs to be reassessed in the light of both Bernal's ideological case, and Renfrew's socio-economic one, allowing for greater flexibility in determining linguistic and cultural boundaries on the one hand (taking into account the Near East and North Africa), and, on the other, for more rigour in pursuing the significance of continuity within one language: as Renfrew points out (167), Mycenaean Greek stands closer to modern Greek than it does to Latin, despite the gap of almost three and a half millennia.

There are three important corollaries for Hellenism today. First, classical philologists can no longer afford to disparage or ignore prehistoric or post-Classical Greece. Second, Byzantinists and neohellenists are freed from the sterile constraints of the post-Fallmerayer debate, which has continued until recently (especially at inaugural lectures in leading British universities): how "Greek" was the Byzantine Empire? how "pure" are the modern Greeks, and what right have they to lay claim to the Byzantine and ancient heritage?[9] Third, Greeks can view their own past with greater detachment and confidence, without need to exclude or apologise for "non-Greek" influences which inevitably occurred—with gains and losses—during the periods of Byzantine, Venetian, and Ottoman rule. The modern Greek repudiation of the Turkish part in its history and culture is the small-nation equivalent of—and predictable response to—the Western repudiation of the Egyptian and Phoenician contributions to ancient Greek civilisation.

To conclude on a positive note, Philology must broaden its horizons by going back to its most ancient sense, "love of argument and reasoning," "love of learning and literature," to include oral as well as written texts, to re-unite the practitioners and theorists of literature, to re-impose the integrity of poetry and music (never lost in Greece, or in many other non-Western cultures), and to admit the beauty and diversity of human cultural interaction. As the Nobel prize-winning Greek poet, Odysseas Elytis, once said, every culture, especially as it gets older, needs "intravenous infusions of civilisation serum" from younger and stronger ones.[10] If such a development seems to threaten entrenched academic disciplines, then so be it. At least one leading neurologist, Oliver Sacks, has faced up to the same dilemma in the medical sciences, when he states, towards the close of his book *A Leg to Stand On*:

> Neuropsychology, like classical neurology, aims to be entirely objective, and its great power, its advances, come from just this. But a living creature, and especially a human being, is first and last *active*—a subject, not an object. It is precisely the subject, the living 'I', which is being excluded. Neuropsychology is admirable, but it excludes the *psyche*—it excludes the experiencing, living 'I'.[11]

If the medical sciences can challenge established disciplinary boundaries, so can philology.

Harvard University

NOTES

1. Nicholas Bachtin, "The Classical Tradition in England," in *Lectures and Essays* (Birmingham: U of Birmingham P, 1963) 125.

2. Nicholas Bachtin, *Introduction to Modern Greek* (Cambridge: UP, 1935) 11–15.

3. George Thomson, " 'Simplex Ordo' and 'The Intrusive Gloss,' " *Classical Quarterly* 15 (1965): 232–43.

4. Dimitris Tziovas, *The Nationism of the Demoticists and its Impact on their Literary Theory, 1880–1930* (Amsterdam: A. Hakkert, 1986) 18–57.

5. Cited by Dennis Baron, *Grammar and Gender* (New Haven: Yale UP, 1986) 13–16.

6. George Thomson, *The Greek Language* (Cambridge: W. Heffer, 1966) 17–18.

7. *Lexikon Archeion tes Meses kai Neas Ellenikes* 2 (1916): 12–48. These cases are cited by Brian Joseph, "European Hellenism and Greek Nationalism: Some Effects of Ethnocentrism on Greek Linguistic Scholarship," *Journal of Modern Greek Studies* 3.1 (1985): 87–96.

8. For a hostile review of Renfrew, which nevertheless fails to address the major arguments, see Marija Gimbutas in *The Times Literary Supplement* (London: Times Newspapers, June 24–30, 1988): 714. From yet another perspective, Mikhail Bakhtin (brother of Nicholas) has argued persuasively that theories of literary change must take account of the "interanimation of languages" and of the "complex and centuries-long struggle of cultures and languages," *The Dialogic Imagination* (Austin: U of Texas P, 1981) 82–83.

9. For details and discussion of the debate, see Margaret Alexiou, "Modern Greek Studies in the West: Between the Classics and the Orient," *Journal of Modern Greek Studies* 4.1 (1986): 3–15.

10. Odysseas Elytis, *First Things First*, trans. Olga Broumas, *American Poetry Review* 17 (January–February 1988): 7.

11. Oliver Sacks, *A Leg to Stand On* (London: Picador, 1984) 164.

Philology as Subversion: The Case of Afro-America[1]

CAROLIVIA HERRON

Philology is the love of the literary word of origin, the love of the cultural language from which contemporary literary art derives. Philology is subversive. Philology is the most effective and thoroughgoing method for persuading classicists, and professors of English literature, and upholders of literary canons, and even radical French literary theorists, that the time has come to include such Afro-American writers as Richard Wright and Toni Morrison in everyone's literary world.

For Afro-America there are two sources for *philologos,* two sources of the literary word of origin, two cultural languages from which contemporary Afro-American literary art derives: the word of Africa, and the word of Europe. The study of these words proceeds under two major afflictions: the word of Africa is essentially unknown, and the word of Europe is essentially unacknowledged and unaccepted.

In my recent visits to Central Africa, to Lubumbashi and Kinshasa in Zaïre, and to Brazzaville, Congo, I have discovered the fundamental and incontrovertible psychic level of the cultural interconnections between Africa and Afro-America—interconnections I have been told repeatedly do not exist. Yet on many evenings in villages outside of Lubumbashi I was struck by the ways in which the rise and fall of speech I could not understand, the manner in which the young people stood by the walls of their houses and talked in the evenings, the movement of their facial expressions, transported me suddenly to my grandmother's house on the outskirts of Washington, D.C. in the summer. I am convinced that there is a profound interconnection between that scene in Zaïre and Afro-American evenings in the United States, but no anthropologist or prophet has yet explained that interconnection—indeed, many of them do not admit that it exists. These African interconnections inform contemporary Afro-American literature, but the philologos, the word of Africa, is unknown.

The philologos of Europe is unacknowledged and unaccepted. Phillis Wheatley (c. 1754–84), the young African slave brought to Boston in 1761, whose poetry founded Afro-American literature, had extensive familiarity with the Homeric epics. Kept as a companion for Mrs. Susannah Wheatley, taught to read and write both English and Latin by the daughter of the family, Mary, Phillis Wheatley showed an early affinity for the Homeric epics as translated into English by Alexander Pope, read Latin poetry in the original, and indeed completed several translations from the works of Ovid. The Homeric epics were her favorite books, and through her dialogue with them she expressed her incipient desire to create an African or an Afro-American epic. One of Wheatley's earliest poems, "To Maecenas," takes the classical epics of Greece and Rome as the context in which she reveals her desire to create great African epic poetry.

The desire to tell the epic tale of Africa in the New World and to assert interconnections with the philologos of Europe is a fundamental aspect of Afro-American literature but is virtually unacknowledged and unaccepted. There appears to be nothing more startling to classicists and Afro-Americanists alike than a presentation of the facts of classical connections in Afro-American literature and culture. While radical breakers of traditional literary canons insist upon their rights to study the periphery of literature—the exclusions of the third world literatures, women, irregular genres such as slave narratives—for Afro-American literature the most radical statement we can make is that Phillis Wheatley loved to read Latin poetry, that Melvin Tolson's epic, A Gallery of Harlem Portraits, is structurally developed from the Homeric epics, that in Derek Walcott's epic poem, Another Life, the hero Gregorias, has received his name, the Greek, through Walcott's admiration of Homer, that there is an entire subgenre of Afro-American literature that has Dante's Commedia as model, that there is a post-bellum genre of Afro-American epic modelled on Milton, Shelley, and others, that if literature belongs to those who use and love it, then Homer, Vergil, Dante, and Milton—these emblems of the philologos of

Europe—belong to Afro-America. Furthermore, the mere description of the philological interconnections between classical European and Afro-American literature is a political method for bringing African and Afro-American literature before the minds and considerations of those who hold the power of canonical reading lists in their hands.

I cannot persuade Miltonists to read African epics by jumping up and down on the table and shouting that you ought to read *Mwindo* or *Sunjiata.* But through philological tools I can demonstrate that the African oral epic, *Ham-Bodêdio,* was composed in a manner that illuminates the manner in which Milton dictated *Paradise Lost.* Miltonists are too curious about Milton to stay away from scholarship such as this—they are compelled by their own love of Milton to consider African epic.

This is my philological method for uniting pleasure with political activism in literary studies. I read epics because I love them—Classical and African and Afro-American and Latin American and Renaissance. And in reading these epics, identifying and analyzing the connections in language, psychology, convention, source, I am able to develop scholarship that brings the have and have-nots of literature face to face. The method by which Ishmael Reed in the twentieth century controverts European Renaissance tradition has an affinity to the method by which Apollonius, in second century B.C. Alexandria, alters the fundamental assumptions of the Homeric epics. Gloria Naylor's inclusion of a radical female component in *Linden Hills,* her novel having Dante's *Inferno* as a model, presents a stimulating and I would insist aesthetically pleasing argument on the nature of Western art.

The list of interconnecting works is inexhaustible and profound and leads to the answer to "What Next?" What's next for Afro-American literature is for all of us to look at what has been with us all the time. If you want a contemporary literature with profound and inescapable interconnections with classical philology, we have it. If you want an utterly new literary interconnection with non-European literary cultures, we have it. The two words, Europe and Africa. As Derek Walcott writes in "A Far Cry From Africa,"

> I who am poisoned with the blood of both,
> Where shall I turn, divided to the vein?
> I who have cursed
> The drunken officer of British rule, how choose

Between this Africa and the English tongue I love?
Betray them both, or give back what they give?
How can I face such slaughter and be cool?
How can I turn from Africa and live?[2]

Harvard University

NOTES

1. Since writing this paper, I have been reconsidering the philosophies of dichotomy (primarily between Europe and Africa) in theories of African-American culture. Although this paper refers extensively to such concepts of cultural dichotomy, I am convinced that this division of African-American culture into two sources, while providing convenient labels for canonical changes in pedagogy, restricts and detracts from the complexities of African-American culture. I treat this issue at length in the chapter "Unreliable Dichotomies" from *Classic Blacks: African American Epic Tradition from Homer to Harlem*, which is Volume I of *African-American Epic Tradition* forthcoming from Stanford UP.

2. Derek Walcott, *Collected Poems 1948–1984* (New York: Farrar, Straus, & Giroux, 1986) 18.

Past and Future in Classical Philology

RICHARD F. THOMAS

If as one of the aims of philology we may include the establishment of knowledge about literary texts, it will be useful, before attempting to define and talk about the future of philology, to discuss its past, specifically to focus on a few products of classical scholarship which all satisfy the following: they have been produced by philologists, represent the best of their type, and have advanced our knowledge about the texts which they treat. In each case, however, we will see that there is some failing, but further that these failings do not matter, for succeeding generations of philologists were to refine and correct, and thus to improve the state of knowledge and continue the process of inquiry. In each case we will also see that the process is still incomplete, that the work is still "in progress" from the point of view of the collective philological community.

Let us confine the list to works on Virgil produced chiefly at the beginning of this century and the end of the last. First, O. Ribbeck who, in his critical editions of 1859–62 and 1894–95, collated both the late antique capital and the Carolingian manuscripts, collected the citations of Virgil in the ancient authors, and assembled conjectures of scholars up to his own time. Ribbeck provided a foundation for subsequent work, as is eloquently stated in the two editions ultimately succeeding him and currently in use.[1] So Mynors, whose first edition is separated from Ribbeck's by more than a century, demonstrates how timeless is the philological world. His familiarity with Ribbeck is immediate, and seems to belie the intervening years: "Especially I thank Otto Ribbeck; it is hard to put into words how much he has contributed to the study of Vergil."[2] And yet this same Ribbeck "without applying any method either deleted or transposed lines of Vergil (a vice of almost all philologists of that day)."[3] But that does not vitiate Ribbeck's accomplishment, for the subsequent tradition merely took what was "good" and "right" from his work (of which there was much) and modified or discarded what was not "good" and "right." And the process is still incomplete; for C. Murgia is preparing a new critical edition for the Teubner (Stuttgart) series.

One of the great commentaries on a Latin literary work is that of E. Norden on book 6 of the *Aeneid*.[4] The information, from Greek and Latin literature, and from elsewhere, presented by Norden to elucidate this part of the poem, is daunting, and his commentary, in its fifth edition, is the starting point for all scholarship. That said, it must be said too that frequently Norden's commentary, although it may teach its reader something, may not answer the question with which the reader approached it; and secondly it fairly consistently refuses to confront or satisfactorily to discuss literary issues. That is in the nature of commentary, and it is in the nature of great literary works that no commentary can provide all the answers to the questions that such works generate. And so, although Norden's commentary is still reprinted in its fifth edition, there is another commentary to which our putative reader will also go, that of R.G. Austin,[5] and it will come as no surprise that this too is to be supplemented by a forthcoming commentary, to be produced by F.M. Ahl. The result of all of this, building on Norden's work (which itself built on an existing tradition of commentaries) will again be a philological collective, still not exhausting the questions this literary text generates, but attempting to increase our knowledge about it. And from this collective future philologists will select, reject, and modify.

The year 1903 saw not only the first edition of Norden's commentary but also the first of Richard Heinze's *Vergils epische Technik*.[6] Some 60 years later Brooks Otis could say of this work, which no contemporary of Heinze's would have excluded from a definition of philology, "in respect to the *Aeneid* as a whole there is still no book or general treatment that has anything like the importance of Heinze's great work."[7] As Otis notes, one of Heinze's chief achievements was the demonstration of the un-Homericness of Virgil's narrative technique, that in "*psychological* and *dramatic* emphasis [it was] different from all Greek epic of which we know"

(414). But Heinze tended to treat technique as a separable element, rather than as an integral part of the movement of the poem, and avoided questions of interpretation. Otis' criticism (414) is curiously close to Geymonat's of Ribbeck: "This, however, was a limitation peculiar to Heinze's time." As in the two preceding *exempla,* there followed modification of and building on Heinze's work, chiefly with the study of V. Pöschl,[8] and later with the monumental work of G.N. Knauer.[9] This latter in particular is of relevance to the present discussion. Knauer for 359 pages continues the interpretive discussion of Virgilian technique, but in the last 160 he gives two lists: one of lines of the *Aeneid* referring to Homer, and a second of lines of Homer influencing lines of the *Aeneid.* Why? Because as Knauer realizes, the process of examining Virgil's technique, as a phenomenon in its own right and in connection with the tradition of Homeric technique, is still in progress. Side by side with interpretation and criticism, we find a philological tool or resource for subsequent philological inquiry, in this case of an interpretive type. And given the current critical interest in narratology,[10] we may expect Knauer's work to be put to new use, which, again, will further diversify and invigorate this area of classical philology.

Here then, are some acknowledged examples of the "best" in philology from the last century or so. In each case flaws were purged by the subsequent tradition. What of "bad" philology? Quite simply, like the flawed elements of good philology, this too gets corrected. Be it through the invective of a Housman preface, the process of reviewing, the testing ground of the seminar and professional conference, sometimes just through silence, the process of correction and adjustment asserts itself. Bad philology is still a part of philology, and is absorbed by it, perhaps even contributing in the process as it makes us confront the reasons for its being bad. The same may be said about the attack on philology, be it by Nietzsche, by the aestheticist tradition,[11] or, more recently, by feminists and by theoreticians. While the notion that philology is to be considered "logocentric," or, worse, "phallogocentric," and is therefore a conceptually impossible or politically unconscionable activity will not find favor with practitioners of philology, the philosophically or ideologically legitimate components of such suggestions will compel (and have already done so) philologists to address questions of fixity of language, intentionality, canon formation, and the like. In the process philology is enriched and further diversifies itself.

How then do we define philology? Perhaps we can do no more than define it by paraphrase of its constituent parts, that by philology is meant the conducting of a φιλία (*philia*) relationship (that is, in a relationship of "affection," "respect," and "close proximity") to the λόγος (*logos*) (that is, the "word," or the "text"). The end or goal of this relationship may be seen as the following: philology believes, or philologists believe, that there are historical, objective truths about language and literature, and that, however great the obstacles, these truths may be reached, or at least approached, through a wide variety of methods.[12]

Obviously with such a definition the term philology has wide coverage: it is a component of textual criticism and editing, the writing of commentaries, stylistic and metrical studies, as well as those modes of interpretation and literary history wherein the notions of "affection," "respect," or "close proximity" to the text are maintained.[13] At the same time it draws from history, archaeology, palaeography, epigraphy, historical linguistics, anthropology, the study of religion, and critical theory, for all of these potentially aid in the quest for facts and truths about literary texts. In short it is an oddity that in current discussions philology is somehow held to be narrow, whereas it seems to me it is as broad as the questions that its texts generate. Within the field of Classics this breadth can be demonstrated by the variety of Ph.D. topics written at Harvard under the rubric "Classical Philology" (these are collected in the back of *Harvard Studies in Classical Philology*), and for that matter by the variety of articles in that periodical itself, or in *Classical Philology* or *American Journal of Philology*. I am not suggesting that all such dissertations and articles are philology, but I am suggesting that many of them employ philology to a greater or lesser degree. Arrowsmith[14] claimed that "what mattered to Nietzsche was the Classics, not philology." But in Nietzsche's world there hardly existed literary criticism and interpretation, so it is difficult simply to resurrect, as Arrowsmith does, the hostility that Nietzsche felt—the target has changed identity and expanded.

Philology, defined thus as a relationship of "affection," "respect," and "close proximity" to a "text," necessarily involves reverence on the part of the critic towards the text; that is, it involves a separation of literature and criticism, as being distinct in kind and therefore beyond competition. Here we find ourselves in potential conflict with recent, chiefly deconstructionist, critical theory, whose goal, in the words of R. Tallis, is "to dominate rather than to interpret literature."[15] Or, in the words of one more sympathetic to deconstruction: "the reader or critic shifts from the role of consumer to that of producer."[16] But these are boundaries which for philology are uncrossable. The attempt to cross them is not a matter of devilishness and potency (as the deconstructive critic might see it), but a conceptual impossibility and a grotesquery.

Nor should this be taken as blind resistance or hostility to theory,[17] although it does imply a reasoned hostility to a certain *type* of theory.[18] What I am really suggesting is that deconstruction is something "other" than philology, in that it denies *prima facie* that there is any truth about language, that things can be "known" about literary texts, so in a sense deflects even the attempt that is at the heart of philology. Such a mode is not so much to be "excluded" from the realm of philology, for by the very nature of its foundation it has already willingly excluded itself. It is interesting, however, that de Man attempts to appropriate philology to poststructuralism in his essay "The Return to Philology."[19] But few philologists will see much with which to identify in his version of it. But other theoretical models such as New Criticism, structuralism, reader response theory, or New Historicism (which looks quite a lot like old historicism) all have the potential to contribute to philology.

What, then, of the future? My own expertise is in the field of classical philology, and here the health of the future is sound, with conditions. It depends first on remaining secure in the face of what are essentially pressures from the outside, and specifically pressures to be new and innovative, because in the marketplace that the academy has become "newness" and "innovation" are in and of themselves deemed desirable. In Latin the word *nouus* means not only "new," but "unfamiliar," "surprising," and "strange." New is not always good or desirable to the classical philologist in the same way it is to the social scientist—who is perhaps responsible for creating these very pressures. If there is such a thing as "truth" in language and literature, it need not follow that access may be had to that truth only by novelty. At the same time university administrators must distinguish differences in groups such as the following: "new blackboard," "new building," "new computer"/"new theory," "new culture," "new literature."

Likewise the soundness of the future depends on confronting the question of relevance, confronting it neither defensively nor tendentiously, allowing that classical philology is no longer and should no longer be the centre of the curriculum as it was for the nineteenth century, but arguing with equal insistence that these cultures and these literatures (understanding of which is, again, the aim of classical philology), in spite of being representative of Western thought, have something to teach us, that they are worth reading and thinking about.

That said, a few thoughts, necessarily superficial, on why there are still things to be done in classical philology. First, there is the fact that there *is* novelty: there are new materials. Classical philology has a surprising advantage over English philology in that over the last century we have had a reasonably steady stream of papyrological finds consisting in part of poetry which, in distinction from the new materials in English literature, is a product of a traditional literary culture, and which therefore not only awaits interpretation but also assists interpretation of texts which have existed for some time. For instance, before 1927 we did not know the programmatic import of Virgil's Sixth eclogue, because we were unaware that it "translated" and reapplied the poetics of the beginning of Callimachus' *Aetia*. Only since 1977 have we been able to appreciate fully Virgil's career shift as presented at the beginning of the third book of the *Georgics*, for in that year the corresponding part of Callimachus' same poem, the *Aetia*, came to light, and Virgil clearly responds to it. Or, purely within Greek literature, the corpus of the best of the New Comic poets, Menander, has been expanding over the last century, and continues to expand even now, yielding substantial fragments and even complete plays.

At the same time the canon has been made more flexible and opened up, as happens in the course of time and as tastes change. So Ovid, the most prolific of the Roman poets, is right now probably the most written-about of the Roman poets, and whereas he used to be regarded in some classicizing circles as a tedious and facile rhetorician, endlessly repeating artificial truisms, he is now widely held to be much more sophisticated in terms of metaphor, narrative method, and genre renovation, in areas, that is, where philology has recently been expanding its interests. Similar things can be said about Seneca. The *Georgics* of Virgil held great interest to the seventeenth and eighteenth centuries, but not much to the nineteenth and, until recently, the twentieth. And the basis of its current appeal is not coincident with the basis in those earlier ages. Few bothered to read the Greek novel two decades ago; this summer at Dartmouth College there will be a week-long conference purely on this topic, with 90 papers scheduled!

There are also new technologies, chiefly produced by computers.

Global word-searching from all of Greek and Latin literature, searching for clusters of words, for metrical patterns and stylistic patterns, and similar philolgical procedures, can now be done in minutes and hours—where the nineteenth-century scholar spent years of toil. Of course we still must be sure to ask the right questions, so such machines are only the tools of philology, and can never be more. Clearly philological training (that is, thorough grounding in the languages and immersion in the literature, history, and culture of the ancient world) is a prerequisite for asking of the right questions, and much of the work done with computers to date has merely confirmed the intuition and labor of philologists, intuition based on profound linguistic, metrical, and stylistic *knowledge,* the result of philological training.

But, more important, even without the aid of specific theories there are always new ways of approaching our literature, new understandings of its mechanics and cultural basis. An obvious example is in Homeric studies, where the findings of Parry and Lord are still being refined and accommo-dated to other more conventional modes of Homeric criticism. Or, in the criticism of Greek tragedy, where anthropology or the study of religion and of ritual behavior have helped our understanding of the cultural and religious setting of the literature. Or, in Latin poetry, the further we get from Romanticism, the less we read the lyric and elegiac poetry of Rome as a purely personal and spontaneous form, and the more receptive we become to its metaphorical levels, its treatment of poetics, and so on. Similarly, the more we understand about the creative aspects of allusion and reference—and this understanding likewise involves a distancing from Romanticism—the less we view Latin literature as an appendix to Greek, and the more we appreciate its creativity.

In short, I would pronounce classical philology alive and well, and predict a healthy future. Philology takes what it wants from wherever it wants—from theory, from technology, from a number of other, evolving disciplines—and brings it to bear on the text. This is what makes it so difficult to define, and it is in this that its continued evolution is guaran-teed. The task of classical philology is to continue to enquire into the literature of these cultures, and to strive towards the facts that may be known about them. The texts themselves, and the questions those texts generate, will do the rest.

Harvard University

NOTES

1. Those of R.A.B. Mynors (1969; Oxford: Oxford UP, 1980) and M. Geymonat (Torino: Paravia 1973).

2. Mynors xiii: "Gratias ago in primis Ottoni Ribbeck, qui quantum studiis Vergilianis tribuerit, difficile est dictu." Cf. also Geymonat ix.

3. Geymonat ix: "nullo adhibito modo, Vergili versus vel deleret vel transponeret (quae erat fere omnium illius aetatis philologorum libido)." Geymonat, I hasten to add, mentions this only in a concessive clause, otherwise sharing Mynors' enthusiasm.

4. E. Norden, *P. Vergilius Maro, Aeneis Buch VI*, 5th ed. (1903; Stuttgart: B.G. Teubner, 1970).

5. *P. Vergili Maronis Aeneidos Liber Sextus* (Oxford: Oxford UP, 1977). Its scope and aims are very different from those of Norden.

6. Curiously, both books went into their fourth edition in 1957; Heinze's was most recently reprinted in 1965, and is still in print.

7. B. Otis, *Virgil, A Study in Civilized Poetry* (Oxford: Oxford UP, 1964) 414.

8. *Die Dichtkunst Virgils: Bild und Symbol in der Aeneis*, 3rd ed. (1950; Berlin: de Gruyter, 1977).

9. *Die Aeneis und Homer. Studien zur poetischen Technik Vergils mit Listen der Homerzitate in der Aeneis* (Hypomnemata 7 [1964], 2nd ed. 1979).

10. The philologist in me flinches as I employ this hybrid, but philologists are flexible and the word is convenient.

11. Represented well by W. Arrowsmith in his 1963 translation of Nietzsche's attack: "it is only confusion or arrogance about the limits of philological method that . . . allows philologists now to claim that they 'welcome' literary criticism in classical studies; but when it comes to graduate studies, promotions, research and hiring it is clear that what counts in most places is philology." "Nietzsche on Classics and Classicists (Part II)," *Arion* 2 (1963) 9, n. 3. This is telling, for quite clearly in current parlance literary criticism and interpretation are considered a fundamental part of classical philology, chiefly in the United States, but in Europe also. It is philology that has broadened itself to incorporate such elements, presumably in part in response to criticism such as Arrowsmith's.

12. It is, I think, precisely at this point that a parting of company occurs between on the one hand those who would see such truth-seeking as intolerable and simplistic positivism (deconstructionists), and on the other those (among others philologists) who would stop short of seeing complexity of language as necessarily implying nihilistic chaos.

13. In exclusionary terms I am here thinking of excessive aestheticism. This potentially parts company with philology, because the focus is frequently something external to the text—which tends to serve merely as a prompt to uncontrolled, subjective, and personal discussion. In this regard P. de Man is able in his assault on aestheticism ("The Return to Philology," in *The Resistance to Theory* [Minneapolis: U of Minnesota P, 1986] 25), but the alternative is not necessarily deconstruction. Indeed philology has long targeted excessive aestheticism, which may be regarded as that mode which takes over when the critic's eye strays from the text to the effect the text is producing on his emotional (uncritical) state—when his φιλία relationship with the λόγος is disrupted.

14. Above, n. 11, 12.

15. *Not Saussure* (Basingstoke and London: Macmillan, 1988) 9.

16. T. Eagleton, *Literary Theory. An Introduction* (Minneapolis: U of Minnesota P, 1983) 137.

17. And the charge of "hostility" is too frequently levelled by the theoretician against

the non-theoretician, whereas, even if only through the accumulation of such charges, the hostility seems often to proceed in the other direction. As Professor Simon notes in his essay, writers of textual or severely philological dissertations do not, contrary to the implications, consistently get hired in preference to those more concerned with interpretation.

18. So, for instance, one would not exclude all of structuralism from the realm of philology, since it still allows authorial involvement in meaning, and lacks the linguistic nihilism of much deconstructive theory. In this regard as in others there is a qualitative distinction between the theoretical world before and after deconstruction.

19. P. de Man 21–26. Perhaps the basis is in the "close reading" that is claimed to characterize much deconstructive criticism, and which de Man links to the methods for instance of Reuben Brower—methods which would qualify as philological criticism as we are defining it: "He (Brower) was much more interested in Greek and Latin literature than in literary theory" (23). But R. Tallis has well pointed out how, even with Derrida, these "close readings" are "often characterised by his alighting upon a small part of a text— frequently a throwaway remark—and inflating its significance out of all proportion" (170). It is the aim of philology to avoid such selection of straw men. On this see also Eagleton 133.

Philology's Discontents: Response

STEPHEN OWEN

We cannot help but be struck by the quest of Carolivia Herron's poets to discover the "parent word," the word of origin. It is part of the problematic history of our own civilization that these Afro-American poets become interesting in precisely the way that they are interesting: there is a suspicion abroad that their love of their original word is the love of a word not their own, not the word of their own origins, as if it were someone else's word misappropriated—"unacknowledged and unaccepted" in Herron's words. Yet we may be far too complacent about other versions of this project: we find that, every time we press the quest to its limit the original word can never be our own, never recreated, appropriated, or even grasped. The more we loved the word, the more it finally eluded us somewhere. The early philologists did not realize this; but the history of the discipline has made it obvious: the certainties of the last century are too often this century's quaint anecdotes, proving to us once again how much wiser we are than our forebears. If philology has a present and a future, it must involve some mature humor about the helplessness of its passion.

I mean this in a very pragmatic and untheoretical way. And to illustrate I would like to offer a few words in praise of the philological sophistication of my own field, traditional Chinese literature, where, already in the seventeenth century, modern philological research was developing out of traditional exegetical practices (basic philological procedures can be

traced back to the first century B.C.; here I am speaking of a philology
that we would all recognize as "modern"). Radical skepticism of received
interpretations and procedures for questioning and adjudicating plausible
philological issues in texts have over the past few centuries attained a
certain maturity in the Chinese tradition—*kào-cheng hsüeh*—and this maturity may point the way for us to the future of philology in our own
civilization. Philology flourished in many areas, but its real perfection was
perhaps realized in scholarship on the *Shih ching,* the classic *Book of Odes.*
There I think we can say with some pride that three centuries of superb
philology has made the book totally unreadable for any serious scholar. In
virtually every poem of that ancient collection a good scholar can read
only multiple possibilities, and this experience is given flavor by the clear
certainty that only one of those possibilities can be correct. Word X is
either a certain kind of plant, the sail of a boat, a sleeping mat, or an
exclamation suggesting intense passion. Eternal verities dangle by very
fragile strings from tenuous structures of philological argumentation. Recently published commentaries that hope to be read by ordinary people
have learned to wisely ignore three centuries of philological advances.

I recall that in a *Rig Veda* course I took as an undergraduate we were
reading comfortably along, following our professor's direction. Then toward the middle of the term he sent us out to look at all the scholarly
translations of one particular hymn. We came back to the next class:
"But, professor, it seems that no two of them have anything in common
with any of the others." "Yes," answered the professor, "and they are all
wrong." After which he proceeded to give us his right interpretation.

These are parables for philology in this late age of the world—even
though my parables are based on old and linguistically problematic works
that pose the problem of understanding words in a radical way, they are
not irrelevant to understanding any text. To be blunt, philology began as
a recognition that the text is "other," not immediate, and not immediately one's own. Such estrangement from the text can lead to the discov-
ery of connections that were not previously apparent, as in the epics that
Carolivia Herron discusses in her essay. Yet this hard-won position of
distance led to an act of critical questioning that was *inherently* desta-
bilizing. Philology may have developed procedures and a particular rhetori-
cal tone in order to try to restabilize what it set adrift, but it initiated that
group of intellectual procedures we now call "criticism" in a number of
fields. Philology's promise to compensate for its disruptions by providing

more reliable truths was ultimately nothing more than a promise; and the numerous claims of a final arrival at truth have proved far less durable than the act and procedures of questioning. Now we are beginning to understand that if we take it seriously, philology and its strange children offer us greater understanding, but no peace.

Rather than being opposed to criticism, philology is more justly opposed to a certain aspect of pedagogy. Pedagogy has its own worthy motives and social imperatives: in teaching we are compelled to pretend that we understand certain things that we really do not understand all that well. Philology, on the other hand, is an austere discipline that keeps pedagogy honest. Certainly in my own field—and I do not think it is unfair to say the same has been true in biblical and classical scholarship— philology has been the deadliest enemy of eternal verities. The realities of language are unkind to easy notions of truth—though those same realities of language do a pretty good job of reminding us how the human mind works. One sentence in Richard Thomas' essay particularly strikes me: in commenting how he had been resettled in New Haven by a reviewer, he adds "And the fact is that the reading I had given Virgil allowed the possibility of a less stable and absolute text than had existed previously— which is, I suppose, true of any new interpretation." Amen. Good philology is and has been tremendously discomforting—not by design, but by its honesty. Later, offering us a philological unsettling of our first year Latin book, Thomas reminds us that *novus* is a newness that may also be threatening, and in the same breath he tells us that such newness may not be desirable to the classical philologist, as opposed to the institutional demand for innovation. If he unsettled the stability of Virgil in his interpretation, I suppose it was because he could not help it: *novus*. I like this as a characterization of philology: it is a reluctantly perpetual innovation that believes with all its heart in stability and is in search of stability. In loving the original word we find that it is not our own, cannot be easily appropriated and processed into a quick verity for Tuesday's class, no matter whether the verity is a new one or a familiar old one. There are those in the easy verities camp who claim philology as their own, as a mantle of their virtue. I don't know what texts they have been reading, but I don't think they deserve the name.

Philology is *not* opposed to *some* of the recent movements in literary studies; philology *caused* them, and they are responses to that problem that inheres in the very concept of the discipline: the reflective questioning of the texts that can be at peace only when it discovers something stable, and therefore will never be at peace. Impressive acts of erudition can lead us to believe that we have found peace in certain disputed matters of words (there are too many impressively erudite scholars in my field, who can persuasively muster great bodies of textual support for positions that are mutually exclusive). If one questions words honestly and bravely, one must accept the consequences of the act, however uncomfortable: somehow in that process one comes always at last to determinations which are of crucial importance but which cannot be known with certainty; and one reaches that point by the very procedures of philology; questioning, we come to a level that is more fundamental than the last, but at which the criteria of validation that philology uses to stabilize its questioning are no longer adequate. I would agree with Thomas that tossing all determinations back to the reader would be beyond the world of philology; but I frankly don't really think people who make such a claim really mean what they say; rather I think the gesture is an attempt to find some grounding for the peculiar experience of not being able to come securely home to the word.

When I say this, I have no intention at all of being nihilistic or pessimistic. I think it is simply a fallacy—and a remarkably odd fallacy at that—to assume that understanding more and better will mean that one's understanding is more secure. We have a choice between the pedagogical verity and philological doubt, and we will with all probability do a little of both. The philological disposition will not make us happier or make more obedient citizens of our students. I find it spiritually fortifying to articulate at least one eternal verity a day; but when I do I always raise my eyes from the page. There is no doubt that philology looks for solid ground; but the very fact that it looks so intently for solid ground should tell you exactly where it is and where it is going. It is, my friends, criticism without shore, and, like it or not, we have already embarked.

Harvard University